Children's and Young Adult Literature by Latino Writers:

A Guide for Librarians, Teachers, Parents, and Students

Sherry York

Linworth
PUBLISHING, INC.

Library of Congress Cataloging-in-Publication Data

York, Sherry, 1947-
    Children's and Young Adult Literature by Latino Writers : a guide for librarians, teachers, parents, and students / by Sherry York.
        p. cm.
    Includes bibliographical references and index.
    ISBN 1-58683-062-7
        1. American literature--Hispanic American authors--Bibliography. 2. Hispanic Americans--Juvenile literature--Bibliography. 3. Hispanic Americans in literature--Bibliography. 4. Young adult literature, American--Bibliography. 5. Children's literature, American--Bibliography. 6. Hispanic Americans--Bibliography. I. Title.

Z1229.H57 Y67 2002
[PS153.H56]
016.8108'09282'08968--dc21

2002067112

Published by Linworth Publishing, Inc.
480 East Wilson Bridge Road, Suite L
Worthington, Ohio 43085

Copyright © 2002 by Linworth Publishing, Inc.

ISBN 1-58683-062-7
5 4 3 2 1

In memory of
Matilde, Brenda, and Christina—
Three bright spirits.

About the Author

Sherry York worked as an educator in Texas schools for 29 years before retiring. During her career, she taught English, language arts and reading, directed a Right to Read program, worked as a school librarian, completed an in-house automation of a library and served on two public library boards. She also conducted faculty in-service programs, served on district and regional committees, started and sponsored two student literary magazines and reviewed books for several magazines and journals. York and her husband Donnie, also a retired librarian, now reside in Ruidoso, New Mexico.

Acknowledgments:

My heartfelt thanks to Joan Haberkorn, a fellow librarian who supplied valuable input and useful suggestions; to Donna Miller, whose editing guidance is always helpful and tactful; to Marlene Woo-Lun, who has given me the opportunity to write reviews and articles for the past 20 years; and to Donnie York, whose support means everything.

Table of Contents

Chapter 1

Introduction

What is a Latino? A Latino is a person (female or male) whose cultural heritage is related to the Spanish language. A Latino may be a Mexican American whose ancestors have lived in the United States since the colonial days. A Latino may be a Mexican American whose ancestors came to the United States from Mexico during the Mexican Revolution era of the early twentieth century.

A Latino may be a Puerto Rican born in the commonwealth of Puerto Rico or the descendent of a Puerto Rican native. A Cuban citizen who left Cuba when Castro gained control of that country is a Latino as are other Cubans who came to the United States for any reason. The child, grandchild, or great-grandchild of a Cuban emigrant is a Cuban American and a Latino.

Latinos may be immigrants from Mexico, Central America, South America, the Caribbean, or Spain. Latinos may be the descendants of immigrants from any of those places. Regardless of how individual Latinos came to be in the United States, Latinos are a valuable resource.

The fact that you are reading this book indicates that you have some interest in Latino literature for children and young adults. Whether you are a librarian, a teacher, a parent, or a student, this guide is for you.

Purpose

Statistics indicate that the Latino population is increasing rapidly and that Latinos are living, working, and **reading** all across the United States. This guide is designed to help librarians, teachers, parents, and students learn and teach about Latinos and find appropriate reading materials by Latinos.

For librarians, this book provides publication and review information to guide in the acquisition process. Librarians should keep in mind that this is emerging literature and should balance a desire for quality with the need to provide authentic Latino-authored literature. It is possible to censor by imposing impossibly high standards, as in the case of the high school librarian in a district with over 60 percent Latino students whose only book by a "Latino" was *Don Quixote*.

The titles in this guide are in print and available for purchase at this time. As librarians know, many books go out of print, some never to return. However, librarians also know that books that are selling well are less likely to go out of print. It should be noted that some titles in this guide are being rebound and are available in that format.

For teachers, this guide will serve as a selection tool for finding titles to suggest to school and public librarians or to purchase for classroom use. In schools that use computerized testing programs like Accelerated Reader from Renaissance Learning or Reading Counts from Scholastic, teachers may be interested in knowing whether or not computer tests are available for specific titles. Individual entries in the guide indicate if a test now exists. Both programs continue to expand, so titles currently without tests may have tests added in the future. Teachers are reminded that the selection of tests available at each school varies. Simple existence of a test does not necessarily mean that it is available at every school. This guide may be used as the basis for requesting the purchase of additional computerized tests for the school. Both Reading Counts and Accelerated Reader Web sites allow teachers and librarians to recommend titles for test development to meet user needs. Librarians and teachers should take advantage of the opportunity to add diversity to those programs.

Teachers are encouraged to read as many of the titles as possible to become familiar with more books, authors, and cultures. Increased awareness will pay dividends in classroom teaching. By including Latino literature in social studies, science, mathematics, and other subjects, teachers will be supporting an improved school climate. If standardized test scores are a consideration, then an accepting school climate, improved reading and writing skills, and critical thinking and higher-level thinking are important. Teachers can use this guide, read Latino literature, and integrate Latino literature into their teaching.

When students are required to become active participants in the learning process and encouraged to be creative and to use their unique talents and capabilities, real learning can occur. Latino-authored literature can easily be incorporated into this active learning process. "Copy-proof" assignments that require a process leading to the creation of a product might include:

▶ written documents such as reports, e-mail messages, letters, scripts for radio or television commercials, interview transcripts, student-made tests, or literary critiques

▶ oral presentations such as reports, dramatic readings, or book talks

▶ audio or video recordings of interviews, conversations, announcements, or programs

▶ multimedia presentations such as infomercials or television-style documentaries

▶ works of art such as posters, collages, drawings, paintings, or sculptures

▶ performances such as interpretive dances, skits, or musical performances

▶ group projects such as panel discussions or debates

▶ computer-generated products such as programs, graphics, charts, or graphs

▶ projects such as bulletin boards or book displays

▶ creative writings of stories, poems, newspaper articles, or journals

▶ creative products such as time lines, map biographies, travel brochures, Web pages, a "zoo" of animals, or a "botanical garden" of a locale, and

▶ how-to demonstrations such as preparing a recipe or planning a quinceañera celebration.

With a willing attitude, teachers can use Latino-authored literature to enrich the learning process in individual classes and to engage other teachers in cross-curricular lessons that encourage broader thinking and critical thinking. Such endeavors hopefully will improve school climates, engage students in meaningful learning, discourage dropouts, and improve student achievement.

Parents may be interested in children's and young adult literature for a variety of reasons. Latino parents may wish to share their cultural heritage with their children. Parents of any culture may wish to encourage their children to be accepting of all cultural groups. Parents may want to expand their own awareness of the diverse groups of our multicultural society. Some parents would like to share the reading experience with their children. Many books in this guide are excellent resources for reading discussion groups.

Parents in community and religious organizations may find the folklore section, with its list of professional Latino storytellers, useful. Parents who home school their children may be concerned about insuring that their children develop and maintain a connection to society outside the home environment. This guide can help in any of these areas. The material in this guide is presented in a straightforward manner without educational or technical jargon. It is not necessary to read the entire text to obtain needed information.

Students of any age can formulate a learning and reading plan to gain a greater understanding of Latino literature. Students may wish to begin by reading works by a specific author or ethnic group. Another approach might be to sample works from several ethnic groups and compare and contrast those works according to historical experiences or geographical location. Learning about Latino literature should be an enjoyable experience. As students read and discover new and interesting books and authors, it is hoped that they will share this experience with friends, teachers, librarians, and family.

Criteria for Inclusion

Materials selected for this guide are by U.S. Latino writers. In cases where the designation "Latino" is somewhat questionable, the practical working definition for the purposes of this guide was, "if the writer considers herself or himself Latino, then she or he is." As our population becomes increasingly diverse through generations of intermarriage between cultural and racial groups, there are often no simple answers to the question, "What are you?"

Most books in this guide were written for children or young adults. A few exceptions were made for works that the author felt will have a special appeal to young adults. Chapter 10 lists notable Latino authors who have written for general audiences. Some potentially useful resources for teachers and parents have been included in the resources section even though they are not written for children or teens. Numerous picture books by Latino writers are listed in the author's *Picture Books by Latino Writers: A Guide for Librarians, Teachers, Parents, and Students* (Linworth Publishing, Inc. 2002) and, therefore, have not been included in this guide.

Although the author, an experienced librarian, teacher, and reviewer, has read the books, listened to the audiotapes, and viewed the videotapes, she has not attempted to rate or disqualify any works based on personal or professional evaluations. Because each reader brings different experiences and requirements to the reading process, the author has attempted to provide enough information so that each individual can make an informed decision about reading or purchasing these materials. Listings of review sources have been provided whenever possible. Information also has been included about prestigious awards that titles have received. The author is not recommending these titles, but is recommending that librarians, teachers, parents, and students consider these titles.

Format

Books in this guide include novels and chapter books, short stories, folklore, drama, poetry, and nonfiction. Information for individual books includes title and author. Spanish book titles are capitalized as printed in the books except titles in all capitals have been changed. Accents on Spanish names have been included according to accents used in the books. Other information includes Library of Congress numbers (LC#), editions with International Standard Book Number (ISBN) and format, paperback (pb), hardcover (hc), or library binding (lib. bdg.). Description section provides number of pages, size in centimeters (cm), and illustration information. Number of chapters is provided for fiction books with chapters. Available Library of Congress summaries and subject headings are included.

The interest level(s) designations are based on various reviews and publishers. Readers will often find that more than one age or interest range is indicated. As experienced teachers and librarians know, determination of interest level is an imprecise art. Individual students vary greatly in maturity levels, interests, and reading preferences at any age or grade level. Interest level is simply a guess as to what the "average" child will enjoy reading.

Reading levels also vary greatly within the pages of a novel or story. Reading levels in this guide are based on information from Scholastic and Renaissance Learning and from other publishers. Often reading levels differed, so all numbers were included. The primary purpose of determining the reading level of a work is to avoid the frustration children may experience when trying unsuccessfully to read a work that is beyond their comprehension level. In some cases, a child's interest in a particular work may enable the child to read "above level," so these numbers should be considered merely a general guide.

Reviews from professional journals are indicated in the reviewed section. The reviews themselves cannot be included because of copyright considerations. Those concerned with professional evaluations of a work may wish to locate and read reviews. Readers should realize that professional reviewers frequently disagree. It is important to read reviews critically and to consider whether their concerns coincide with the reader's.

Major awards that a book has received are indicated. Pertinent awards in this field are the Américas, Pura Belpré, and Tomás Rivera. Several organizations such as the American Library Association, Children's Book Council, National Council of Teachers, and other groups provide annual lists of recommended books. Some titles from state reading lists also are included.

The tests category indicates the existence of Accelerated Reader (Renaissance Learning) or Reading Counts (Scholastic) tests. Notes refer to additional information relevant to the book and its contents. Web sites that contain useful specific information about individual books are included. The genre of a novel is given if it was listed in the Library of Congress. Setting is provided only in cases where it is not easily discerned from the book's summary and subjects if the author of this guide felt that setting has potential relevance. Series titles are provided as applicable. Contents listing are included as appropriate for short story, folklore, and drama collections.

Title:
Author:
Translator: (if applicable)
Publication:
LC#:
Editions:
Description:
    Chapters: (if applicable)
Summary:
    Series: (if applicable)
    Contents: (if applicable)
Subjects:
    Genre: (if applicable)
    Setting: (if applicable)
Interest Level:
Reading Level:
Tests:
Reviewed:
Awards:
Lists:
Note:

Format of book descriptions

Chapter 2 consists of novels and chapter books, and Chapter 3 contains short stories. Chapter 4 includes books of folklore, multicultural storytellers, and a listing of audio cassettes and CDs. Latino-authored drama books are listed in Chapter 5. Poetry and anthologies are found in Chapter 6. Chapter 7 contains nonfiction; resource materials are included in Chapter 8. Chapter 9 contains brief biographical information about authors. Chapter 10 lists other Latino writers whose works are for general or adult audiences. Appendix A contains a listing of some non-Latinos closely associated with Latino literature. Appendix B lists relevant publishers with addresses, telephone and fax numbers, and Web sites.

Students, teachers, and parents are encouraged to read Latino literature and suggest and recommend titles to school and public librarians. The author hopes that all librarians, teachers, parents, and students will find this a useful tool, will enjoy reading these books as much as she has, and that each reader will in time become a promoter of Latino literature.

While this guide attempts to include all Latino-authored children's and young adult books currently in print, it is inevitable that some titles will be omitted either through oversight or because of publishing schedules. The author apologizes in advance for unintentional omissions and is delighted that new books in this field are appearing with increasing frequency.

A Brief History of Children's and Young Adult Literature by Latinos

U.S. Latinos have had a difficult time getting their literature into print. That fact is especially true for U.S. Latino writers of children's and young adult literature. Even standard reference works about Latino writers have contained almost nothing about young adult and children's literature primarily because such literature was almost nonexistent.

Dr. Isabel Schon pioneered in the field with her reference books for teachers and librarians. However, the focus of her early books was on books written in Spanish or translations into Spanish of Anglo-authored books. Few of the titles featured in *Books in Spanish for Children and Young Adults* (Scarecrow 1978–1993) and *Recommended Books in Spanish for Children and Young Adults* (Scarecrow 1997, 2000) were by U.S. Latino writers since most were writing in English. Likewise, her *Hispanic Heritage* series books (Scarecrow 1980–1997) only recently began to include a significant number of Latino writers from the United States.

Therefore, information included in this brief history is, of necessity, based on Library of Congress records, examination of authors' publishing careers, and personal observations made during the author's career that began in 1969. At the present time, a specific history of children's and young adult literature by U.S. Latino writers has yet to be written, as far as could be ascertained from the author's research.

U.S. Latino-authored children's and young adult literature basically did not exist before the 1970s when Puerto Rican Nicholasa Mohr published *Nilda* (1973), *El Bronx Remembered* (1975), *In Nueva York* (1977), and *Felita* (1979). There were no English-language children's or young adult books by Mexican Americans or Cuban Americans. Some Spanish-language children's books were available, but most were translations from English and were not by U.S. Latino writers.

During that same decade, Tejano Tomás Rivera's *...And the Earth Did Not Part/...y no se lo tragó la tierra* (1971) and New Mexican Rudolfo Anaya's *Bless Me, Ultima* (1972) were published by Quinto Sol of Berkeley, California. Both titles are now considered classics of Chicano literature. Like Piri Thomas' *Down These Mean Streets* (1967) and Sandra Cisneros' *House on Mango Street* (1985), these titles were embraced by those seeking Latino authors and were placed on school reading lists although the books were not actually written for children or teens.

During the 1980s, Mohr was joined by Gary Soto (*The Cat's Meow*, 1987) from Strawberry Hill Press and Irene Beltrán Hernández (*Across the Great River*, 1989) from Arte Público Press. Arte Público's Piñata Books imprint was established in 1994 and continues to publish Hispanic authors. The nonprofit Children's Book Press of San Francisco began a concerted effort to publish picture books that were relevant to minority children.

During the 1990s, pioneers of children's and young adult literature were joined by Cubans Alma Flor Ada and Anilú Bernardo, Puerto Ricans Judith Ortiz Cofer, Marisa Montes, Esmeralda Santiago, and Carmen T. Bernier-Grand, and Mexican Americans Diane Gonzales Bertrand, Ofelia Dumas Lachtman, and Gloria Velásquez. Victor Martinez received a National Book Award for his first novel, *Parrot in the Oven*. The first novels of Francisco Jiménez (*The Circuit*) and Floyd Martinez (*Spirits of the High Mesa*) gained notice.

Pam Muñoz Ryan, David Rice, René Saldaña, Kathy Balmes, and other Latinos were publishing fiction for younger readers as the new century began. Pat Mora, Juan Felipe Herrera, Luis J. Rodríguez, and Gary Soto produced poetry and picture books for children and teens. Several Latinos published short story collections, picture books, folklore, and plays for younger readers. A few Latino-authored biographies and other nonfiction works began to appear.

Veronica Chambers, a Panamanian American, Julia Mercedes Castilla, a Colombian American, and Julia Alvarez, a Dominican American, added diversity to the group of Latino authors. Books by Chambers, Gerald and Janice Haslam, and other Latinos reflected the reality that many children and young adults are of mixed heritage or ethnicity.

It is tempting to look at the cumulative lists of fiction, short stories, folklore, drama, poetry, and nonfiction by Latino writers and become complacent. The reality is that these titles represent almost 30 years of publishing history, and the number of Latino authors of children's and young adult literature is miniscule.

As our society becomes increasingly diverse, it is essential that all young readers have access to literature that reflects their cultures. Young readers must be able to read about others like themselves in order to learn to accept and appreciate those who are different. Exposure to literature by Latino authors can help Latino children and teens develop a sense of cultural pride. Exposure to literature by Latino writers can help all children and teens develop an appreciation of Latino cultures and a sense that we are all more alike than we are different. In the complex society of the twenty-first century, we must recognize and value the diversity of cultures that make up our country.

Chapter 2

Latino Novels and Chapter Books

Books included in this chapter are novels and shorter works of fiction sometimes referred to by teachers as "chapter books." Chapter books are usually somewhat longer than picture books and are divided into several chapters.

In the following pages librarians seeking to add Latino-authored fiction to their collections will find more than fifty fiction books available for purchase. Teachers seeking novels or chapter books should find useful titles in this chapter. Parents and students of Latino literature should find ample choices of fiction based on Mexican American, Cuban, Puerto Rican, and other Latino characters in a variety of geographical locations in the United States. These fiction titles include both historical and contemporary settings.

Short stories will be found in Chapter 3. Biographical information about the authors will be found in Chapter 9. Chapter 10 contains additional authors who have written books of adult fiction and fiction for general audiences.

Across the Great River

- **Author:** Irene Beltrán Hernández
- **Publication:** Houston, TX: Arte Público Press, 1989
- **LC#:** 89000289
- **Editions:**
  0934770964 pb.
- **Description:** 136 pages, 22 cm. Cover illustration by Mark Piñón.
- **Chapters:** 10
- **Summary:** Katarina Campos and her family are separated while illegally crossing the border from Mexico to Texas.
- **Subjects:**
  Emigration and immigration—Fiction
  Immigrants—Texas—Fiction
  Mexican Americans—Fiction
- **Interest Level:** young adult
- **Reading Level:** 4.3
- **Tests:** Accelerated Reader
- **Reviewed:** *The Book Report, Booklist, ALAN Review, San Francisco Chronicle*
- **Lists:** *Brave Girls and Strong Women*
- **Web site:**
  <www.unigiessen.de/~ga52/seminarP/mcyal98/grRiver.htm>
  <http://ladb.unm.edu/retanet/plans/search/retrieve.php3?ID[0]=442>
- **Note:** Features a female protagonist.

Alicia's Treasure

- **Author:** Diane Gonzales Bertrand
- **Publication:** Houston, TX: Piñata Books, 1996

- **LC#:** 95037669
- **Editions:**
  1558850856 hc. Arte Público
  1558850864 pb. Arte Público
  0613179587 hc. Econo-Clad
- **Description:** 123 pages, 23 cm. Illustrated by Daniel Lechón.
- **Chapters:** 13
- **Summary:** When ten-year-old Alicia accompanies her brother and his girlfriend to the beach, she experiences many things for the first time and gains new insights into herself.
- **Subjects:**
  Beaches—Fiction
  Brothers and Sisters—Fiction
  Mexican Americans—Fiction
- **Interest Level:** ages 8–12, 9–12, grades 3–4, 4–6
- **Reading Level:** 3.9
- **Tests:** Accelerated Reader
- **Reviewed:** *Booklist, Horn Book*
- **Awards:** Tomás Rivera nominee 1996

Breaking Through

- **Author:** Francisco Jiménez
- **Publication:** Boston: Houghton Mifflin, 2001
- **LC#:** 2001016941
- **Editions:**
  0618011730 hc.
- **Description:** 208 pages, 19 cm.
- **Chapters:** 25
- **Summary:** Having come from Mexico to California ten years ago, fourteen-year-old Francisco is still working in the fields but is

fighting to improve his life and complete his education.
- ▶ **Subjects:**
  Agricultural laborers—Fiction
  California—Fiction
  Mexican Americans—Fiction
  Mexican Americans—Juvenile fiction
- ▶ **Interest Level:** grades 5–8, 6–12
- ▶ **Reviewed:** *Booklist, Publishers Weekly, School Library Journal*
- ▶ **Note:** Sequel to *The Circuit*

Buried Onions

- ▶ **Author:** Gary Soto
- ▶ **Publication:** San Diego, CA: Harcourt Brace, 1997, 1st edition
  New York: HarperCollins, 1999, 1st paperback edition
- ▶ **LC#:**
  96053112 Harcourt
  98053886 HarperCollins
- ▶ **Editions:**
  0152013334 hc Harcourt
  0064407713 pb. HarperCollins
  0788752669 audio book Recorded Books, 2001
- ▶ **Description:** 149 pages, 22 cm. Cover illustration by Peter Tovar. Harcourt
  149 pages, 21 cm. Cover illustration by Mike Benny. HarperCollins
- ▶ **Chapters:** 9
- ▶ **Summary:** When nineteen-year-old Eddie drops out of college, he struggles to find a place for himself as a Mexican American living in a violence-infested neighborhood of Fresno, California.

- ▶ **Subjects:**
  Mexican Americans—Fiction
  Violence—Fiction
- ▶ **Interest Level:** ages 12–14, 12 & up, young adult
- ▶ **Reading Level:** 5.3, 5.9
- ▶ **Tests:** Accelerated Reader, Reading Counts
- ▶ **Reviewed:** *Booklist, Kirkus, Horn Book, Publishers Weekly, School Library Journal, VOYA*
- ▶ **Awards:** Américas commended 1997
- ▶ **Lists:** ALA Best Books for Young Adults, ALA Popular Paperbacks for Young Adults nominee 2002, ALA Quick Picks for Reluctant Young Adult Readers, Capitol Choices, Noteworthy Books for Children, Garden State Teen Book Awards 2000, Texas Lone Star 1998–1999, 1999–2000, Texas Tayshas 1998–1999
- ▶ **Web site:** <http://harperchildrens.com/rgg/rggburied1.htm>
- ▶ **Note:** Includes a glossary of Spanish words and phrases.

Call Me Consuelo

- ▶ **Author:** Ofelia Dumas Lachtman
- ▶ **Publication:** Houston, TX: Arte Público Press, 1997
- ▶ **LC#:** 96050201
- ▶ **Editions:**
  1558851879 pb. alk paper Arte Público
  1558851887 hc. alk paper Arte Público
  0613179617 lib. bdg. Econo-Clad
- ▶ **Description:** 149 pages, 22 cm. Illustrated by Daniel Lechón (cover) and Virginia Roeder (interior).

- ▶ **Chapters:** 17
- ▶ **Summary:** After suddenly being orphaned, twelve-year-old Consuelo reluctantly moves in with her American grandmother while hoping to return soon to her Mexican American family.
- ▶ **Subjects:**
  Grandmothers—Fiction
  Mexican Americans—Fiction
  Moving, Household—Fiction
- ▶ **Interest Level:** ages 8–12, 9–12, young adult
- ▶ **Reading Level:** 3.7
- ▶ **Tests:** Accelerated Reader
- ▶ **Reviewed:** *Horn Book, School Library Journal*
- ▶ **Awards:** Tomás Rivera nominee 1997
- ▶ **Lists:** California Booklist: Books Set in Los Angeles, Hollywood, and Surrounding Areas, New York Public Library's Books for the Teen Age

The Cat's Meow

- ▶ **Author:** Gary Soto
- ▶ **Publication:** San Francisco, CA: Strawberry Hill Press, 1987
  New York: Scholastic, 1995
- ▶ **LC#:**
  87017982 Strawberry Hill
  95004311 Scholastic
- ▶ **Editions:**
  0590470019 hc. Scholastic
  0894070878 pb. Strawberry Hill
  0590470027 pb. Little Apple
  0613074513 lib. bdg. Econo-Clad
- ▶ **Description:** 64 pages, 20 cm. Illustrated by Carolyn Soto (Strawberry Hill)

78 pages, 21 cm. Illustrated by Joe Cepeda (Scholastic)
- ▶ **Chapters:** 7
- ▶ **Summary:** Eight-year-old Nicole, who is part Mexican, is amazed when her cat Pip starts speaking in Spanish.
- ▶ **Subjects:**
  Cats—Fiction
  Mexican Americans—Fiction
  Spanish language—Fiction
- ▶ **Interest Level:** ages 4–8, 9–12, grades 1–5
- ▶ **Reading Level:** 2, 3.2
- ▶ **Tests:** Reading Counts
- ▶ **Reviewed:** *Booklist, Kirkus, School Library Journal*
- ▶ **Note:** A beginning chapter book
- ▶ **Note:** Includes a glossary.
- ▶ **Note:** Spanish version, *Maullido de la gata* 061309803X from Scholastic, is not currently available.

The Children of Flight

Pedro Pan

- ▶ **Author:** María Armengol Acierno
- ▶ **Publication:** Kaleidoscope Press, 1994 New York: Silver Moon Press, 1994
- ▶ **LC#:** 9347651
- ▶ **Editions:**
  18818899521 Silver Moon hc.
- ▶ **Description:** 76 pages, maps, 24 cm. Cover illustration by Nan Galub.
- ▶ **Chapters:** 8
- ▶ **Summary:** In 1961, ten-year-old María and her younger brother face an uncertain future

after they arrive in Miami from Cuba without their parents.

▶ **Subjects:**
Cuban Americans—Fiction
Miami (Fla.)—Fiction

▶ **Setting:** Cuba and Florida, 1961

▶ **Series:** Stories of the States

▶ **Interest Level:** ages 9–12, middle grades

▶ **Reading Level:** 5.0

▶ **Tests:** Accelerated Reader, Reading Counts

▶ **Reviewed:** *Midwest Book Review, School Library Journal, Small Press*

▶ **Web site:**
<www.silvermoonpress.com/assets/PDFs/StoriesOfTheStates/TGUIDE-PedroPan.pdf>

▶ **Note:** Includes a historical postscript by Robert M. Levine, Professor of History and Director of Latin American Studies, University of Miami, pages 70–76.

▶ **Note:** Includes a bibliography.

The Circuit: Stories from the Life of a Migrant Child

Cajas de carton

▶ **Author:** Francisco Jiménez

▶ **Publication:** *The Circuit*. University of New Mexico Press, 1997
The Circuit. Houghton Mifflin, 1999
Cajas de carton. Houghton Mifflin, 2000

▶ **LC#:** 97004844

▶ **Editions:**
0826317979 pb. University of New Mexico Press, *Circuit*

0395979021 hc. Houghton Mifflin, *Circuit*
0613068033 lib. bdg. Econo-Clad, *Circuit*
1883332710 unabridged audio CD, Audio Bookshelf, *Circuit*
1883332443 unabridged audio cassette, Audio Bookshelf, *Circuit*
0395955815 pb. *Cajas*
1883332729 unabridged audio CD, Audio Bookshelf, *Cajas*
1883332451 unabridged audio cassette, Audio Bookshelf, *Cajas*

▶ **Description:** 134 pages, 18 cm. Cover illustration Susan Marquez (UNM Press)
Chapters: 12

▶ **Summary:** Twelve autobiographical stories about the life of Francisco Jiménez as he and his parents worked in the fields of California.

▶ **Subjects:**
California—Social life and customs—Fiction
Mexican-American families—Fiction
Mexican Americans—Fiction
Migrant agricultural laborers—Fiction

▶ **Interest Level:** grades 4–8, 5–9

▶ **Reading Level:** 5.3, 5.5

▶ **Tests:** Accelerated Reader, Reading Counts

▶ **Reviewed:** *Booklist, Horn Book*

▶ **Awards:** Américas 1997, 1998 *Boston Globe-Horn Book* Award for fiction, 1998 California Library Association John and Patricia Beatty Award, 1998 Jane Addams Children's Book Award Honor book

▶ **Lists:** ALA Best Books for Young Adults, ALA Popular Paperbacks for Young Adults, *Booklist* Editors' Choice 1997, Young Hoosier Award

CrashBoomLove:

A Novel in Verse

- ▶ **Author:** Juan Felipe Herrera
- ▶ **Publication:** Albuquerque: University of New Mexico Press, 1999
- ▶ **LC#:** 99006603
- ▶ **Editions:**
  0826321135 hc.
  0826321143 pb.
- ▶ **Description:** 155 pages, 22 cm.
- ▶ **Chapters:** None.
- ▶ **Summary:** After his father leaves home, sixteen-year-old César García lives with his mother and struggles through the painful experiences of growing up as a Mexican American high school student.
- ▶ **Subjects:**
  High school—Fiction
  Mexican Americans—Fiction
  Mexican Americans—Juvenile fiction
  Schools—Fiction
- ▶ **Interest Level:** young adult
- ▶ **Reading Level:** 6.5
- ▶ **Tests:** Reading Counts
- ▶ **Reviewed:** *Booklist, School Library Journal*
- ▶ **Awards:** Américas award winner 1999, Latino Literary Hall of Fame 2000
- ▶ **Lists:** ALA Best Books for Young Adults nominee, ALA Quick Picks for Reluctant Young Adult Readers, ALA "Top List of 2000," *Los Angeles Times* Book Prize finalist, New York Public Library's Books for the Teen Age
- ▶ **Note:** Individual poems make up the novel.

Don't Spit on My Corner

- ▶ **Author:** Miguel Durán
- ▶ **Publication:** Houston, TX: Arte Público Press, 1992
- ▶ **LC#:** 91029104
- ▶ **Editions:**
  1558850422 pb. Arte Público
  0785718656 lib. bdg. Econo-Clad
- ▶ **Description:** 187 pages, 22 cm. Cover design by Mark Piñón.
- ▶ **Chapters:** 26
- ▶ **Summary:** Pachuco "Little Mike" grew up in East Los Angeles during World War II, dressed cool, hung out, cruised, boozed it up, and protected his turf.
- ▶ **Subjects:**
  East Los Angeles (Calif.)—Fiction
  Mexican Americans—Fiction
- ▶ **Genre:** Bildungsromane
- ▶ **Interest Level:** age 11 & up, young adult
- ▶ **Reading Level:** 5.3
- ▶ **Tests:** Accelerated Reader
- ▶ **Reviewed:** *Kirkus*
- ▶ **Note:** Miguel Durán was a counselor to Luis J. Rodríguez.

Emilio

▶ **Author:** Julia Mercedes Castilla
▶ **Publication:** Houston, TX: Piñata Books, 1999 (English version)
Norma S.A. Editorial, 1997 (Spanish version)
▶ **LC#:** 99029481
▶ **Editions:**
1558852719 pb. Arte Público (English)
9580441499 pb. Norma (Spanish)
▶ **Description:** 105 pages, 22 cm. Cover illustration by Giovanni Mora. (Arte Público)
162 pages pb. (Norma)
▶ **Chapters:** 13
▶ **Summary:** A young immigrant from Central America finds it difficult to learn English and adjust to life in the big city of Houston, Texas.
▶ **Subjects:**
Emigration and immigration—Fiction
Hispanic Americans—Fiction
▶ **Interest Level:** ages 9–12, 12 & up
▶ **Reading Level:** 4.1
▶ **Tests:** Accelerated Reader
▶ **Reviewed:** *Multicultural Review*
▶ **Note:** English and Spanish versions have different settings.

Esperanza Rising

▶ **Author:** Pam Muñoz Ryan
▶ **Publication:** New York: Scholastic Press, 2000
▶ **LC#:** 00024186
▶ **Editions:**
0439120411 hc.
0807262072 audio tape Listening Library
4.5 hours, 3 cassettes, narrator Trini Alvarado
▶ **Description:** 262 pages, 22cm. Cover illustration by Joe Cepeda.
▶ **Chapters:** 14
▶ **Summary:** Esperanza and her mother are forced to leave their life of wealth and privilege in Mexico to go work in the labor camps of Southern California, where they must adapt to the harsh circumstances facing Mexican farm workers on the eve of the Great Depression.
▶ **Subjects:**
Agricultural laborers—Fiction
California—Fiction
Mexican Americans—California—Fiction
Mexican Americans—California—Juvenile fiction
▶ **Interest Level:** ages 9–12, grades 5–8, 5–9
Reading Level: 5.3, 5.5
▶ **Tests:** Accelerated Reader, Reading Counts
▶ **Reviewed:** *Booklist, Horn Book, Kirkus, School Library Journal, VOYA*
▶ **Awards:** Américas honorable mention 2000, Tomás Rivera nominee 2000
▶ **Lists:** ALA Best Books for Young Adults, *L.A. Times* Best Books of 2000, Notable Trade Books in the Field of Social Studies (NCSS-CBC), *Publishers Weekly* Best Children's Books 2000, *Smithsonian* Best Books 2000
▶ **Web sites:**
<http://teacher.scholastic.com/authorsandbooks/authors/ryan/learn.htm>
<http://teachers.eusd.k12.ca.us/jleff/pamryan.html>
▶ **Note:** Based on the life of the author's grandmother. Author's note: pp. 255–262.
▶ **Note:** Esperanza is age 13 when the book begins.

Felita

▶ **Author:** Nicholasa Mohr
▶ **Publication:** New York: Dial Press, 1979
▶ **LC#:** 79050151
▶ **Editions:**
0803731434 hc.
0803731442 lib. bdg.
0141306432 pb. Puffin
0833546619 lib. bdg. Econo-Clad
9993958972 pb. Bantam reissue edition
0553157922 pb. Bantam
▶ **Description:** 112 pages, 22 cm. Illustrated by Ray Cruz.
▶ **Chapters:** 7
▶ **Summary:** This book highlights the everyday experiences of an eight-year-old Puerto Rican girl growing up in a close-knit, urban community.
▶ **Subjects:**
City and town life—Fiction
Puerto Ricans—United States—Fiction
▶ **Setting:** New York City
▶ **Interest Level:** ages 8–12, 9–12
▶ **Reading Level:** 3.6, 4.0, 5.2
▶ **Tests:** Accelerated Reader, Reading Counts
▶ **Reviewed:** *Horn Book, Publishers Weekly, School Library Journal*
▶ **Awards:** American Book Award (Before Columbus Foundation) 1981
▶ **Lists:** Child Study Children's Book Committee Children's Book of the Year, Notable Children's Trade Books in the Field of Social Studies (NCSS-CBC)

Firefly Summer

▶ **Author:** Pura Belpré
▶ **Publication:** Houston, TX: Piñata Books, 1996
▶ **LC#:** 96015679
▶ **Editions:**
1558851747 hc.
1558851801 pb.
0613179641 lib. bdg. Econo-Clad
▶ **Description:** 207 pages, 22 cm. Cover illustration by Kath Christensen.
▶ **Chapters:** 15
▶ **Summary:** At a plantation in rural Puerto Rico around the turn of the century, the foreman pursues the mystery surrounding his family.
▶ **Subjects:**
Puerto Rico—Fiction
▶ **Interest Level:** ages 9–11, 9–12
▶ **Reading Level:** 5.4
▶ **Tests:** Accelerated Reader
▶ **Reviewed:** *The Book Report*
▶ **Note:** Published as a part of the "Recovering the U.S. Hispanic Literary Heritage" project of Arte Público Press.

The Girl from Playa Blanca

▶ **Author:** Ofelia Dumas Lachtman
▶ **Publication:** Houston, TX: Piñata Books, 1995
▶ **LC#:** 95009864
▶ **Editions:**
155851488 hc.
1558851496 pb.
0785784713 lib. bdg. Econo-Clad
▶ **Description:** 259 pages, 22 cm. Cover illustration by Daniel Lechón.

- ▶ **Chapters:** 25
- ▶ **Summary:** When Elena and her little brother, Carlos, leave their Mexican seaside village to search for their immigrant father in Los Angeles, they encounter intrigue, crime, mystery, friendship, and love.
- ▶ **Subjects:**
  Brothers and sisters—Fiction
  Emigration and immigration—Fiction
  Mexicans—United States—Fiction
  Mystery and detective stories
- ▶ **Interest Level:** age 11 & up, 9–12, young adult
- ▶ **Reading Level:** 4.4
- ▶ **Tests:** Accelerated Reader
- ▶ **Reviewed:** *Booklist, Horn Book, The Book Report, School Library Journal*
- ▶ **Awards:** Benjamin Franklin Award for Young Adult Literature

Going Home

- ▶ **Author:** Nicholasa Mohr
- ▶ **Publication:** New York: Dial Books for Young Readers,1986
  Puffin, 1999, reprint edition
- ▶ **LC#:** 85020621
- ▶ **Editions:**
  0141306440 pb. Puffin
  0553156996 pb. Bantam Skylark
  0833529390 lib. bdg. Econo-Clad
- ▶ **Description:** 192 pages, 22 cm. Cover illustration by Jean-Paul Tibbles.
- ▶ **Chapters:** 13
- ▶ **Summary:** Feeling like an outsider when she visits her relatives in Puerto Rico for the first time, eleven-year-old Felita tries to

come to terms with the heritage she always took for granted.
- ▶ **Subjects:**
  Family life—Fiction
  New York (N.Y.)—Fiction
  Puerto Ricans—New York (State)—New York—Fiction
  Puerto Rico—Fiction
- ▶ **Interest Level:** ages 9–12, grades 4–6
- ▶ **Reading Level:** 4.4, 5.8
- ▶ **Tests:** Accelerated Reader, Reading Counts
- ▶ **Reviewed:** *School Library Journal*
- ▶ **Lists:** Notable Children's Trade Books in the Field of Social Studies (NCSS-CBC)
- ▶ **Note:** Sequel to *Felita*

Good Morning Alberto

- ▶ **Author:** Sergio Flores
- ▶ **Publication:** La Puente, CA: Los Andes Publishing Company, 1999
- ▶ **LC#:** NA
- ▶ **Editions:**
  1571590048 pb.
- ▶ **Description:** 121 pages, 22 cm. Illustrated by Edgar Cosio.

- ▶ **Chapters:** 21
- ▶ **Summary:** Alberto Jiménez sometimes wishes his family was different, but when his father becomes ill and loses his job, Alberto begins to value his family and culture.
- ▶ **Subjects:**
  California—Fiction
  Family life—Fiction
  Immigrants—California—Fiction
  Mexican Americans—Fiction
  Poverty—Fiction
  Schools—Fiction
- ▶ **Interest Level:** ages 9–12

Heartbeat Drumbeat

- ▶ **Author:** Irene Beltrán Hernández
- ▶ **Publication:** Houston, TX: Arte Público Press, 1992
- ▶ **LC#:** 91048246
- ▶ **Editions:**
  155885052X pb.
- ▶ **Description:** 134 pages, 22 cm. Cover illustration by Mark Piñón.
- ▶ **Chapters:** 16
- ▶ **Summary:** A young woman finds the course of her life influenced by her Navajo and Mexican heritage and especially by an older Navajo woman and a young Indian lawyer.
- ▶ **Subjects:**
  Indians of North America—Fiction
  Navajo Indians—Fiction
  Navajo Indians—Juvenile fiction
- ▶ **Interest Level:** age 11 & up, 12 & up, young adult
- ▶ **Awards:** Benjamin Franklin Award (Publishers Marketing Association)

How Tía Lola Came to (Visit) Stay

- ▶ **Author:** Julia Alvarez
- ▶ **Publication:** New York: Alfred A. Knopf, 2001
- ▶ **LC#:** 00062932
- ▶ **Editions:**
  0375902155 lib. bdg. Knopf
  0375802150 hc. Knopf
- ▶ **Description:** 147 pages. 22 cm. Cover illustration by Joe Cepeda.
- ▶ **Chapters:** 10
- ▶ **Summary:** After his parents' divorce, ten-year-old Miguel's aunt, Tía Lola, comes to Vermont from the Dominican Republic to stay with him, his mother, and his sister. Although Miguel is at first embarrassed by his colorful aunt, he learns to love her.
- ▶ **Subjects:**
  Aunts—Fiction
  Divorce—Fiction
  Dominican Americans—Fiction
  Family life—Vermont—Fiction
  Vermont—Fiction
- ▶ **Interest Level:** ages 9–12, grades 3–6, 4–7
- ▶ **Reviewed:** *Booklist, Kirkus, Publishers Weekly, School Library Journal*
- ▶ **Note:** An author's note at the end—A Word About the Spanish (Una palabra sobre el español)—explains the differences in Spanish in different locations.

In the Shade of the Níspero Tree

- ▶ **Author:** Carmen T. Bernier-Grand
- ▶ **Publication:** New York: Orchard Books, 1999
- ▶ **LC#:** 98041160
- ▶ **Editions:**
  053101540 hc. Orchard
  0531331547 lib. bdg. Orchard
  0440416604 pb. Young Yearling, reprint edition
- ▶ **Description:** 186 pages, 22 cm. Cover illustration by Raúl Colón.
- ▶ **Chapters:** 23
- ▶ **Summary:** Because her mother wants her to be part of the world of high society in their native Puerto Rico, nine-year-old Teresa attends a private school but loses her best friend.
- ▶ **Subjects:**
  Best friends—Fiction
  Prejudices—Fiction
  Puerto Rico—Fiction
  Schools—Fiction
- ▶ **Setting:** Ponce, Puerto Rico, 1961
- ▶ **Interest Level:** ages 9-12, grades 4-7, 5-8
- ▶ **Reading Level:** 5.0
- ▶ **Tests:** Reading Counts
- ▶ **Reviewed:** *Booklist, Horn Book, Kirkus, Publishers Weekly, School Library Journal*
- ▶ **Lists:** Capitol Choices
- ▶ **Note:** Teresa is in the fourth grade.

Jesse

- ▶ **Author:** Gary Soto
- ▶ **Publication:** San Diego: Harcourt Brace, 1994
- ▶ **LC#:** 94011256
- ▶ **Editions:**
  051240239X hc Harcourt
  0613000161 lib. bdg. Econo-Clad
  0590528378 pb. Point Signature
  0788731661 audio book Recorded Books, 1999
- ▶ **Description:** 166 pages, 22 cm. Cover illustration by Simón Silva.
- ▶ **Chapters:** 19
- ▶ **Summary:** Two Mexican-American brothers hope that junior college will help them escape their heritage of tedious physical labor.
- ▶ **Subjects:**
  Mexican Americans—Fiction
  Universities and colleges—Fiction
- ▶ **Setting:** Vietnam War era, Fresno, California
- ▶ **Interest Level:** grades 7–9, 10–12, young adult
- ▶ **Reading Level:** 5.8, 7.1
- ▶ **Tests:** Accelerated Reader, Reading Counts
- ▶ **Reviewed:** *The Book Report, Booklist, Horn Book, Kirkus, School Library Journal, VOYA*

Jumping Off to Freedom

- ▶ **Author:** Anilú Bernardo
- ▶ **Publication:** Houston, TX: Piñata Books, 1996.
- ▶ **LC#:** 95037667
- ▶ **Editions:**
  1558850872 hc. alk. paper
  1558850880 pb. alk. paper
  0613179706 lib. bdg. Econo-Clad

▶ **Description:** 198 pages, 23 cm. Cover illustration by Gladys Ramirez.

▶ **Chapters:** 10

▶ **Summary:** Courage and desperation lead fifteen-year-old David and his father to flee Cuba's repressive regime and seek freedom by taking to the sea on a raft headed for Miami.

▶ **Subjects:**
Cubans—Florida—Fiction
Cubans—Florida—Juvenile fiction
Refugees—Fiction

▶ **Interest Level:** ages 9–12, 11 & up, grades 7–10

▶ **Reading Level:** 5.1

▶ **Tests:** Accelerated Reader

▶ **Reviewed:** *Booklist, School Library Journal*

▶ **Lists:** ALA Quick Picks for Reluctant Young Adult Readers, New York Public Library's Books for the Teen Age

The Jumping Tree

▶ **Author:** René Saldaña, Jr.

▶ **Publication:** New York: Delacorte Press, 2001

▶ **LC#:** 00060373

▶ **Editions:**
0385327250 hc.

▶ **Description:** 181 pages. Cover illustration by Rafael López.

▶ **Chapters:** 20

▶ **Summary:** Rey, a Mexican American living with his close-knit family in a Texas town near the Mexican border, describes his transition from boy to young man.

▶ **Subjects:**
Family life—Texas—Fiction
Fathers and sons—Fiction

Mexican Americans—Fiction
Mexican Americans—Juvenile fiction
Texas—Fiction

▶ **Setting:** Nuevo Peñitas, Texas

▶ **Interest Level:** ages 9–12

▶ **Reviewed:** *Booklist, Kirkus*

▶ **Note:** The main character, Rey Castañeda, is in the sixth through eighth grades.

Legend of the Red Wolf

▶ **Author:** Valerie Ozeta

▶ **Published:** Eagle Rock, CA: Red Wolf Publishing, 1998

▶ **LC#:** 97092872

▶ **Editions:**
0966168704 pb.
0966168712 pb. 2nd edition

▶ **Description:** 33 pages, 26 cm. Illustrated by Lupe Costa-Costa.

▶ **Chapters:** Not divided into chapters.

▶ **Summary:** When Great Grandfather appears in a vision and tells the legend of the Red Wolf, Tony is inspired to recruit Pete and the other bullies to help him paint a mural in their desert Southwest home town.

▶ **Subjects:**
Bullies—Fiction
Great-grandfathers—Fiction
Hispanic Americans—Fiction
Indians of North America—Southwest, New—Fiction/Juvenile fiction
Red wolf—Fiction
Southwest, New—Fiction
Wolves—Fiction

▶ **Setting:** Southwest United States

▶ **Interest Level:** ages 8–13

Web site: <www.gotwolf.com>

Note: A study guide and thematic unit are available on the Web site, free with purchase of the book

Lessons of the Game

▶ **Author:** Diane Gonzales Bertrand
▶ **Publication:** Houston, TX: Piñata Books, 1998
▶ **LC#:** 98028340
▶ **Editions:**
  155885245X pb.
▶ **Description:** 149 pages, 22 cm. Cover illustration by Giovanni Mora.
▶ **Chapters:** 11
▶ **Summary:** Romance blossoms when student teacher Kaylene finds that the handsome Alex, a friend from her past, is a football coach at her new school. However, she fears that his busy schedule will not let him spend any time with her.
▶ **Subjects:**
  Football—Fiction
  High schools—Fiction
  Schools—Fiction
  Teachers—Fiction
▶ **Interest Level:** ages 11–13, 11 & up, 12 & up, grades 7–10, young adult
▶ **Reading Level:** 5.4
▶ **Tests:** Accelerated Reader
▶ **Reviewed:** *Booklist, Kirkus*
▶ **Lists:** New York Public Library's Books for the Teen Age
▶ **Note:** A revision of an earlier novel, *Touchdown for Love*
▶ **Note:** The main character is Kaylene Morales, a teacher.

Leticia's Secret

▶ **Author:** Ofelia Dumas Lachtman
▶ **Publication:** Houston, TX: Piñata Books, 1997
▶ **LC#:** 97024772
▶ **Editions:**
  1558852085 hc.
  1558852093 pb.
  0613179714 lib. bdg. Econo-Clad
▶ **Description:** 126 pages, 22 cm. Illustrated by Roberta Collier-Morales.
▶ **Chapters:** 14
▶ **Summary:** Until she learns Leticia's shocking secret, eleven-year-old Rosario cannot understand why adults fawn over this enigmatic cousin who does nothing but sit around the house.
▶ **Subjects:**
  Cousins—Fiction
  Death—Fiction
  Secrets—Fiction
▶ **Interest Level:** ages 8–12, 9–12, grades 5–8
▶ **Reading Level:** 3.7
▶ **Tests:** Accelerated Reader
▶ **Reviewed:** *School Library Journal*
▶ **Awards:** Tomás Rivera nominee 1997

The Little Ghost Who Wouldn't Go Away

El pequeño fantasma que no queria irse

- ▶ **Author:** Joseph J. Ruiz
- ▶ **Translator:** Juan S. Lucero
- ▶ **Publication:** Santa Fe, NM: Sunstone Press, 2000
- ▶ **LC#:** 00026575
- ▶ **Editions:**
  086534309 pb.
- ▶ **Description:** 95 pages, 22 cm. Illustrated by Kris Hotvedt.
- ▶ **Chapters:** Not divided into chapters.
- ▶ **Summary:** A young girl in a small mountain community in northern New Mexico wishes to see the ghost of a little boy who has been seen by many others.
- ▶ **Subjects:**
  Ghosts—Fiction
  New Mexico—Fiction
  Spanish-language materials—Bilingual
- ▶ **Setting:** El Rito, northern New Mexico
- ▶ **Interest Level:** grades 2–4
- ▶ **Reviewed:** *School Library Journal*

Little Juan Learns a Lesson

El pequeño Juan aprende una lección:

- ▶ **Author:** Joseph J. Ruiz
- ▶ **Translator:** A. Samuel Adelo
- ▶ **Publication:** Santa Fe, NM: Sunstone Press, 1997
- ▶ **LC#:** 97028150
- ▶ **Editions:**
  0865342679 pb.
- ▶ **Description:** 63 pages, 22 cm. Illustrated by Kris Hotvedt.
- ▶ **Chapters:** Not divided into chapters.
- ▶ **Summary:** When he goes to buy a birthday present for his father on Halloween, Juan learns the importance of behaving in a kind and generous fashion.
- ▶ **Subjects:**
  Behavior—Fiction
  Halloween—Fiction
  Hispanic Americans—Fiction
  New Mexico—Fiction
  Spanish-language materials—Bilingual
- ▶ **Setting:** Lomas, northern New Mexico
- ▶ **Interest Level:** ages 4–8
- ▶ **Note:** English and Spanish versions on facing pages

Lolo and Red Legs

▶ **Author:** Kirk Reeve
▶ **Publication:** Flagstaff, AZ: Rising Moon, 1998
▶ **LC#:** 97049969
▶ **Editions:**
0873586832 hc.
0873586840 pb.
0613158865 lib. bdg. Econo-Clad
▶ **Description:** 112 pages, 21 cm. Cover illustration by Francisco Mora.
▶ **Chapters:** 18
▶ **Summary:** When eleven-year-old Lolo captures a tarantula, it turns an ordinary summer into a series of adventures that take him and his friends beyond their Mexican-American neighborhood in East Los Angeles.
▶ **Subjects:**
Los Angeles (Calif.)—Fiction
Mexican Americans—Fiction
Tarantulas—Fiction
▶ **Setting:** Las Lomitas (neighborhood) of East Los Angeles
▶ **Interest Level:** ages 7–10, 9–12, grades 3–5, 6–8
▶ **Awards:** Américas commended 1998
▶ **Lists:** Notable Children's Trade Books in the Field of Social Studies (NCSS-CBC)
▶ **Note:** Includes a glossary of Spanish words and phrases.
▶ **Note:** Uses the regional Spanish of Southern California.

Lorenzo's Secret Mission

▶ **Author:** Lila Guzmán, Rick Guzmán
▶ **Publication:** Houston, TX: Piñata Books, 2001
▶ **LC#:** 2001034006
▶ **Editions:**
1558853413 pb.
▶ **Description:** 153 pages, 22 cm. Cover illustration by Roberta Collier-Morales.
▶ **Chapters:** 32
▶ **Summary:** In 1776, when fifteen-year-old Lorenzo Bannister leaves Texas and his father's new grave to carry a letter to the Virginia grandfather he has never known, he becomes involved with the struggle of the American Continental Army and its Spanish supporters.
▶ **Subjects:**
Gálvez, Bernardo de, 1746–1786—Fiction/Juvenile fiction
Gibson, George, 1747–1791—Fiction/Juvenile fiction
Identity—Fiction
Orphans—Fiction
Slavery—Fiction
United States—History—Revolution, 1775–1783—Fiction/Juvenile fiction
▶ **Interest Level:** age 11 & up, grades 6–9
▶ **Reviewed:** *Midwest Book Review, School Library Journal*
▶ **Note:** Based on Bernardo de Gálvez and George Gibson, two historical figures.

Loves Me, Loves Me Not

▶ **Author:** Anilú Bernardo
▶ **Publication:** Houston, TX: Piñata Books, 1998
▶ **LC#:** 98026147
▶ **Editions:**
   1558852581 pb. alk. paper
▶ **Description:** 169 pages, 23 cm. Cover illustration by Giovanni Mora.
▶ **Chapters:** 10
▶ **Summary:** While trying to win the attention of a high school basketball star who already has a girlfriend, Maggie, a Cuban American, learns painful lessons about romantic young love.
▶ **Subjects:**
   Best friends—Fiction
   Cuban Americans—Fiction
   High schools—Fiction
   Interpersonal relations—Fiction
   Schools—Fiction
▶ **Setting:** Florida
▶ **Interest Level:** age 11 & up, 12–14, grades 7–10, young adult
▶ **Tests:** Accelerated Reader, Reading Counts
▶ **Reviewed:** *Booklist*, *Kirkus*, *VOYA*
▶ **Lists:** ALA Popular Paperbacks for Young Adults, New York Public Library's Books for the Teen Age, Texas Tayshas 2000-2001

Manuel and the Madman

▶ **Authors:** Gerald W. Haslam and Janice E. Haslam
▶ **Publication:** Walnut Creek, CA: Devil Mountain Books, 2000

Thwack! Pow! Productions (Box 751060 Petaluma, CA 94975-1060)
▶ **LC#:** 99046429
▶ **Editions:**
   0915685116 pb.
▶ **Description:** 206 pages, 22 cm. Cover illustration by Martha Molinaro and Garth Haslam.
▶ **Chapters:** 38
▶ **Summary:** With the encouragement of his aging neighbor, "the Madman," Manuel, half-Anglo and half-Hispanic, faces the challenges of entering junior high school and comes to value his mixed heritage.
▶ **Subjects:**
   Mexican Americans—Fiction
   Mexican Americans—Juvenile fiction
   Racially mixed people—Fiction
▶ **Setting:** Bakersfield, California
▶ **Interest Level:** ages 9–12
▶ **Note:** Includes a Spanish-English glossary.

Marisol and Magdalena:

The Sound of Our Sisterhood

▶ **Author:** Veronica Chambers
▶ **Publication:** New York: Hyperion, 1998
▶ **LC#:** 97034365
▶ **Editions:**
   0786804378 hc.
   0786823852 lib. bdg.
   0786813040 pb.
▶ **Description:** 141 pages, 22 cm. Cover illustration by Tracy Mitchell.
▶ **Chapters:** 17

▶ **Summary:** Separated from her best friend in Brooklyn, thirteen-year-old Marisol spends a year with her grandmother in Panama where she secretly searches for her real father.

▶ **Subjects:**
Best Friends—Fiction
Fathers and Daughters—Fiction
Grandmothers—Fiction
Panama—Fiction
Panamanian Americans—Fiction
Panamanian Americans—Juvenile fiction

▶ **Setting:** Brooklyn and Panama

▶ **Interest Level:** ages 8–12, 9–12, 9–13, grades 5–8, 6–9

▶ **Reading Level:** 5.2

▶ **Tests:** Reading Counts

▶ **Reviewed:** *Booklist, Horn Book, Latina, School Library Journal*

▶ **Awards:** Américas commended 1998

▶ **Note:** Marisol is Latinegra, black and Latina.

My Name Is María Isabel

Me llamo María Isabel

▶ **Author:** Alma Flor Ada

▶ **Translator:** Ana M. Cerro

▶ **Publication:** New York: Atheneum, Maxwell Macmillan, 1993
New York: Aladdin Paperbacks, 1995

▶ **LC#:** 91044910 (English)
94071330 (Spanish)

▶ **Editions:**
0689315171 lib. bdg. Atheneum
068980217X pb. Aladdin (English)
0689319630 hc. (Spanish)
0689810997 pb. Aladdin (Spanish)

0785783504 lib. bdg. (English) Econo-Clad
0613016254 lib. bdg. (Spanish) Econo-Clad

▶ **Description:** 57 pages (English), 60 pages (Spanish), 22 cm. Illustrated by K. Dyble Thompson. Cover illustration by Elizabeth Sayles.

▶ **Chapters:** 10

▶ **Summary:** Third-grader María Isabel, born in Puerto Rico and now living in the United States, wants badly to fit in at school; the teacher's writing assignment, "My Greatest Wish," gives her that opportunity.

▶ **Subjects:**
Moving, Household—Fiction
Puerto Ricans—United States—Fiction
Schools—Fiction

▶ **Interest Level:** ages 7–10, 9–12

▶ **Tests:** Accelerated Reader, Reading Counts

▶ **Reviewed:** *Horn Book, Kirkus, School Library Journal*

▶ **Lists:** ALA Read*Write*Now Suggested Reading List

▶ **Web sites:**
<www.quia.com/tq/126947.html>
[comprehension quiz]
<www.murrieta.k12.ca.us/alta/grade3/maria>
<http://222.washburn.edu/mabee/
booktalks/maria.html> [booktalk]

▶ **Note:** An Aladdin Chapter Book

Nilda

▶ **Author:** Nicholasa Mohr

▶ **Publication:** New York: Harper & Row, 1973
Houston, TX: Arte Público, 1986, rev. edition

▶ **LC#:** 73008046

- ► **Editions:**
  0030243317 lib.bdg. Harper
  0060243325 lib. bdg. Harper
  0934770611 pb. Arte
  9991922091 pb. Arte 2nd. edition
  0833506560 lib. bdg. Econo-Clad
- ► **Description:** 292 pages, 22 cm. Illustrated by the author.
- ► **Chapters:** [27]
- ► **Summary:** A young girl growing up in Spanish Harlem in the 1940s watches the secure world of her childhood years slowly erode away.
- ► **Subjects:**
  New York (N.Y.)—Fiction
  Puerto Ricans—New York (State)—New York—Fiction
- ► **Interest Level:** age 11 & up
- ► **Reading Level:** 4.5, 5.4
- ► **Tests:** Accelerated Reader, Reading Counts
- ► **Reviewed:** *New York Times, School Library Journal*
- ► **Awards:** *New York Times* Outstanding Book of the Year, ALA Best Books for Young Adults
- ► **Note:** With pictures by the author

No Lack of Lonesome

- ► **Author:** Albino Gonzales
- ► **Publication:** Grand Junction, CO: Farolito Press, 2001.
- ► **LC#:** 2001131430
- ► **Editions:**
  0967985524 pb.
- ► **Description:** 131 pages, 22cm. Cover illustration by Ximena Gonzales.
- ► **Chapters:** [54]

- ► **Summary:** Nana, who can neither read nor write, teaches her grandson about the true meaning of poetry.
- ► **Subjects:**
  Authorship—Fiction
  Bilingualism—Fiction
  Grandmothers—Fiction
  Poetry—Fiction
  Schools—Fiction
  Writing
- ► **Interest Level:** young adult
- ► **Lists:** ALA Best Books for Young Adults nominee 2002

Pacific Crossing

- ► **Author:** Gary Soto
- ► **Publication:** San Diego: Harcourt Brace Jovanovich, 1992
- ► **LC#:** 91046909
- ► **Editions:**
  0152591877 hc.
  0152591885 pb.
  0788729705 audiotape Recorded Books
- ► **Description:** 134 pages, 22 cm. Cover illustration by Goro Sasaki.
- ► **Chapters:** 16
- ► **Summary:** Fourteen-year-old Mexican American Lincoln Mendoza spends a summer with a host family in Japan, encountering new experiences and making new friends.
- ► **Subjects:**
  Japan—Fiction
  Mexican Americans—Fiction
- ► **Setting:** San Francisco and Japan
- ► **Interest Level:** ages 8–14, 9–12, young adult

- ▶ **Reading Level:** 4.6, 6.1
- ▶ **Tests:** Accelerated Reader, Reading Counts
- ▶ **Reviewed:** *Horn Book*, *New York Times*, *Publishers Weekly*, *School Library Journal*, *VOYA*
- ▶ **Note:** Includes a glossary of Japanese words and phrases and a glossary of Spanish words and phrases.
- ▶ **Note:** Audiotape won the Audiofile Earphone Award.

Parrot in the Oven: mi vida

El loro en el horno, mi vida

- ▶ **Author:** Victor Martinez
- ▶ **Publication:** New York: HarperCollins Publishers, 1996
- ▶ **Spanish version:** Noguer y Caralt Editores, 1998, Amalia Bermejo, translator.
- ▶ **LC#:** 96002119
- ▶ **Editions:**
  0060267046 hc.
  0060267062 lib. bdg.
  0064471861 pb. reprint edition
  0613066979 lib. bdg. Econo-Clad
  0694700932 audio tape, abridged, Victor Martinez narrator
  8427932383 pb. Spanish version

- ▶ **Description:** 216 pages, 20 cm. (hc.), 18 cm. (pb.)
- ▶ **Chapters:** 11
- ▶ **Summary:** Manny relates his coming-of-age experiences as a member of a poor Mexican-American family in which the alcoholic father only adds to everyone's struggle.
- ▶ **Subjects:**
  Alcoholism—Fiction
  Family life—Fiction
  Mexican Americans—Fiction
- ▶ **Interest Level:** age 12 & up, grades 7–10, young adult
- ▶ **Reading Level:** 6.1, 7.1
- ▶ **Tests:** Accelerated Reader, Reading Counts
- ▶ **Reviewed:** *Booklist*, *Horn Book*, *Kirkus*, *Publishers Weekly*, *School Library Journal*
- ▶ **Awards:** Américas winner 1996, National Book Award for Young People's Fiction 1996, Pura Belpré winner for narrative 1998, Tomás Rivera nominee 1996
- ▶ **Lists:** ALA Popular Paperbacks for Young Adults nominee 2002, New York Public Library's Books for the Teen Age, *Horn Book* Fanfare Honor List, Texas Tayshas 1999-2000
- ▶ **Web sites:**
  <www.harpercollins.com/rgg/rggparrot.htm [discussion guide]
  <www.harperchildrens.com/hch/havesomefun/guides/0064471861.pdf> [guide]
  <www.pbs.org/newshour/bb/entertainment/november96/martinez_11-7.html> [conversation with Elizabeth Farnsworth about National Book Award Nov. 7, 1996]

Pillars of Gold and Silver

- ▶ **Author:** Beatriz Eugenia De La Garza
- ▶ **Publication:** Houston, TX: Piñata Books, 1997
- ▶ **LC#:** 97022161
- ▶ **Editions:**
  1558852069 pb.
  0613179749 lib. bdg. Econo-Clad
- ▶ **Description:** 260 pages, 22 cm. Cover illustration by Gladys Ramírez.
- ▶ **Chapters:** 8
- ▶ **Summary:** While spending the summer with her grandmother in Mexico, Blanca Estela gradually adjusts to small-town life and knows she will miss it when she returns to the United States.
- ▶ **Subjects:**
  Grandmothers—Fiction
  Mexican Americans—Fiction/Juvenile fiction
- ▶ **Setting:** California and Revilla, Mexico in Korean War era
- ▶ **Interest Level:** age 11 & up, grades 9–12, young adult
- ▶ **Reading Level:** 6.3
- ▶ **Tests:** Accelerated Reader
- ▶ **Reviewed:** *Booklist, Library Journal, School Library Journal*
- ▶ **Awards:** Tomás Rivera nominee 1997
- ▶ **Note:** Appendix includes eight songs and games.

Quinceañera Means Sweet Fifteen

- ▶ **Author:** Veronica Chambers
- ▶ **Publication:** New York: Hyperion Books, 2001
- ▶ **LC#:** 00063386
- ▶ **Editions:**
  0786804971 hc.
  0786824263 lib. bdg.
- ▶ **Description:** 192 pages, 22 cm.
- ▶ **Chapters:** 19
- ▶ **Summary:** Eagerly anticipating her Quinceañera, the fifteenth birthday celebration that will signify her adulthood, Marisol is troubled by a lack of money, her mother's new boyfriend, changes in her best friend, and the absence of the father she never knew.
- ▶ **Subjects:**
  Brooklyn (New York, N.Y.)—Fiction
  Family life—New York (State)—New York—Fiction
  Friendship—Fiction
  Panamanian Americans—Fiction
  Quinceañera (Social custom)—Fiction
- ▶ **Setting:** New York
- ▶ **Interest Level:** ages 8–12, 9–12, 11 & up, grades 5–8, 6–9
- ▶ **Reviewed:** *Booklist, School Library Journal, VOYA*
- ▶ **Note:** Sequel to *Marisol and Magdalena*

Rainbow Boys

- **Author:** Alex Sanchez
- **Publication:** New York: Simon & Schuster Books for Young Readers, 2001
- **LC#:** 2001020952
- **Editions:**
  0689841000 hc.
- **Description:** 245 pages. 24 cm.
- **Chapters:** 22
- **Summary:** Three high-school seniors — a jock with a girlfriend and an alcoholic father, a closet gay, and a flamboyant gay rights advocate — struggle with family issues, gay bashers, first sex, and conflicting feelings about each other.
- **Subjects:**
  Alcoholism—Fiction
  Coming out (Sexual orientation)—Fiction
  High schools—Fiction
  Homosexuality—Fiction
  Interpersonal relations—Fiction
  Schools—Fiction
- **Interest Level:** grade 9 & up, young adult
- **Reviewed:** *School Library Journal, VOYA*
- **Web site:**
  <www.alexsanchez.com/YouthLinks.htm>
- **Note:** Contains information, telephone numbers, and Web sites for
  •Organizing a Peer Group
  •Violence and Hate Crimes against Gays and Lesbians
  •Issues with Parents
  •HIV and AIDS
  •Teen Sexuality
  •Gay and Lesbian Teen Suicides
  •Gay and Lesbian Teen Services on the Internet.

Roosevelt High School Series

- **Author:** Gloria Velásquez
- **Publication:** Houston, TX: Piñata Books
- **Interest Level:** age 11 & up, grades 6–9, 7–10, 7–12, young adult

Ankiza

- **LC#:** 00041697
- **Editions:**
  1558853081 hc.
  155885309X pb.
- **Description:** 144 pages, 22 cm. copyright 2000.
- **Chapters:** 21
- **Summary:** When she begins dating a wealthy white senior, Ankiza must face the reactions and prejudices of other students, parents, and school officials.
- **Subjects:**
  African Americans—Fiction
  High schools—Fiction
  Interracial dating—Fiction
  Prejudices—Fiction
  Schools—Fiction
- **Reviewed:** *School Library Journal, VOYA*
- **Awards:** Tomás Rivera nominee 2000
- **Lists:** ALA Popular Paperbacks for Young Adults nominee 2002
- **Note:** Fifth title of the series

Juanita Fights the School Board

- **LC#:** 94004914
- **Editions:**
  1558851151 pb.
- **Description:** 149 pages, 22 cm. copyright 1994.

- ▶ **Chapters:** 27
- ▶ **Summary:** Johnny, the eldest daughter of Mexican farm workers, is expelled from high school, but with the help of a Latina psychologist and a civil rights attorney, she fights the discriminatory treatment and returns, determined to finish school.
- ▶ **Subjects:**
  Discrimination—Fiction
  High schools—Fiction
  Mexican Americans—Fiction
  Schools—Fiction
- ▶ **Reading Level:** 4.4, 5.5
- ▶ **Tests:** Accelerated Reader, Reading Counts
- ▶ **Reviewed:** *Horn Book, Kirkus*
- ▶ **Note:** Includes a glossary.
- ▶ **Note:** First title of the series

Maya's Divided World

- ▶ **LC#:** 94033573
- ▶ **Editions:**
  1558851267 hc.
  1558851313 pb.
  0613179722 lib. bdg. Econo-Clad
- ▶ **Description:** 125 pages, 22 cm. copyright 1995.
- ▶ **Chapters:** 22
- ▶ **Summary:** When a seventeen-year-old Mexican American girl starts getting into trouble as a reaction to her parents' divorce, she is helped by a psychologist who has problems of her own.
- ▶ **Subjects:**
  Divorce—Fiction
  Mexican Americans—Fiction
- ▶ **Reading Level:** 4.6
- ▶ **Tests:** Accelerated Reader
- ▶ **Reviewed:** *American Bookseller, Booklist, Horn Book, School Library Journal*

- ▶ **Note:** Includes a glossary.
- ▶ **Note:** Second in the series

Rina's Family Secret

- ▶ **LC#:** 98003218
- ▶ **Editions:**
  1558852360 hc.
  1558852336 pb.
- ▶ **Description:** 150 pages, 22 cm. copyright 1998.
- ▶ **Chapters:** 24
- ▶ **Summary:** A Puerto Rican teenager describes her family's life with her abusive stepfather in alternating chapters with the story of the counselor who is trying to help them.
- ▶ **Subjects:**
  Family problems—Fiction
  Family violence—Fiction
  High schools—Fiction
  Puerto Ricans—California—Fiction
  Schools—Fiction
- ▶ **Reading Level:** 5.1
- ▶ **Tests:** Accelerated Reader
- ▶ **Reviewed:** *Booklist, Kirkus*
- ▶ **Awards:** Tomás Rivera nominee 1998
- ▶ **Note:** Includes glossary.
- ▶ **Note:** Fourth title in the series

Tommy Stands Alone

- ▶ **LC#:** 95013551
- ▶ **Editions:**
  1558851461 hc.
  155885147X pb.
  0785784705 lib. bdg. Econo-Clad
- ▶ **Description:** 135 pages, 22 cm. copyright 1995.
- ▶ **Chapters:** 23
- ▶ **Summary:** A high school student and mem-

ber of a Mexican-American family struggles with his sexual identity and finally learns that he will not have to stand alone any more.

▶ **Subjects:**
Family life—Fiction
Homosexuality—Fiction
Identity—Fiction
Mexican Americans—Fiction

▶ **Reviewed:** *Booklist, Multicultural Review*

▶ **Web sites:**
<www.colage.org> Children of Lesbians and Gays Everywhere (COLAGE)

▶ **Note:** The story is based on the life of the author's cousin, who died of AIDS.

The Secret of Two Brothers

▶ **Author:** Irene Beltrán Hernández

▶ **Publication:** Houston, TX: Piñata Books, 1995

▶ **LC#:** 95009844

▶ **Editions:**
1558851410 hc.
1558851429 pb.

▶ **Description:** 181 pages, 22 cm. Cover illustration by Gladys Ramírez.

▶ **Chapters:** 14

▶ **Summary:** Beaver Torres gets out of prison determined to look after his brother Cande and make a good life for them both.

▶ **Subjects:**
Ex-convicts—Fiction
Mexican Americans—Fiction

▶ **Genre/Form:** Bildungsromane

▶ **Setting:** Dallas, Texas

▶ **Interest Level:** age 11 & up, grades 7–10, young adult

▶ **Reading Level:** 5.1

▶ **Tests:** Accelerated Reader

▶ **Reviewed:** *Booklist, San Francisco Chronicle, Texas Books in Review*

▶ **Awards:** Américas commended 1995

▶ **Lists:** ALA Quick Picks for Reluctant Young Adult Readers

The Skirt

▶ **Author:** Gary Soto

▶ **Publication:** New York: Delacorte Press, 1992
New York: Bantam Doubleday Dell Books for Young Readers, 1994 reprint edition

▶ **LC#:** 91026145

▶ **Editions:**
0440409241 pb.
0785735291 lib. bdg. Econo-Clad

▶ **Description:** 74 pages, 20 cm. Illustrated by Eric Velásquez.

▶ **Chapters:** 8

▶ **Summary:** When Miata leaves on the school bus the skirt that she is to wear in a dance performance, she needs all her wits to get it back without her parents finding out that she has lost something yet again.

▶ **Subjects:**
Lost and found possessions—Fiction
Mexican Americans—Fiction
Skirts—Fiction

▶ **Setting:** Sanger, California

▶ **Interest Level:** grades 3–4

▶ **Reading Level:** 3.7, 4.7

▶ **Tests:** Accelerated Reader, Reading Counts

▶ **Reviewed:** *Booklist, Choice, Horn Book, Publishers Weekly, School Library Journal*

▶ **Note:** A beginning chapter book

Something Wicked's in Those Woods

▶ **Author:** Marisa Montes
▶ **Publication:** San Diego, CA: Harcourt, 2000
▶ **LC#:** 99058755
▶ **Editions:**
0152023917 hc.
▶ **Description:** 214 pages, 22 cm. Cover illustration by Mitchell Heinze.
▶ **Chapters:** 35
▶ **Summary:** When their parents are killed in an accident, eleven-year-old Javier and his younger brother leave their home in Puerto Rico to go live with their aunt in Northern California, where a ghost from an unsolved crime and Javi's new-found psychokinetic powers make their adjustment all the harder.
▶ **Subjects:**
Brothers—Fiction
California, Northern—Fiction
Ghosts—Fiction
Parapsychology—Fiction
Puerto Ricans—California—Fiction
Supernatural—Fiction
▶ **Setting:** Northern California
▶ **Interest Level:** grades 4–7, young adult
▶ **Reading Level:** 4.6
▶ **Tests:** Accelerated Reader
▶ **Reviewed:** *Booklist, Kirkus, Publishers Weekly*

Spirits of the High Mesa

▶ **Author:** Floyd Martinez
▶ **Publication:** Houston, TX: Arte Público Press, 1997
▶ **LC#:** 96050286
▶ **Editions:**
1558851984 pb.
▶ **Description:** 192 pages, 22 cm. Cover illustration by Consuelo Udave.
▶ **Chapters:** 19
▶ **Summary:** Flavio and his family and friends are beset by changes in their small New Mexican village after electricity and a sawmill bring strangers into their midst.
▶ **Subjects:**
Family life—Fiction
Grandfathers—Fiction
Mexican Americans—Fiction
New Mexico—Fiction
Schools—Fiction
▶ **Setting:** Capulín, New Mexico and Albuquerque, New Mexico
▶ **Interest Level:** age 11 & up
▶ **Reading Level:** 5.1, 5.5
▶ **Tests:** Accelerated Reader, Reading Counts
▶ **Reviewed:** *The Book Report*
▶ **Awards:** Américas (CLASP) commended 1997, Pura Belpré Honor Book 1998, Small Press Books finalist, Tomás Rivera nominee 1997

The Summer of El Pintor

▶ **Author:** Ofelia Dumas Lachtman
▶ **Publication:** Houston, TX: Piñata Books, 2001
▶ **LC#:** 00069281
▶ **Editions:**
 1558853278 pb.
▶ **Description:** 235 pages, 22 cm. Illustrated by Pauline Rodríguez Howard.
▶ **Chapters:** 21
▶ **Summary:** When sixteen-year-old Monica and her widowed father go back to Los Angeles, reluctantly moving from a wealthy neighborhood to the barrio house her mother grew up in, Monica tries to locate a missing neighbor, and in the process learns about her mother's past.
▶ **Subjects:**
 Identity—Fiction
 Los Angeles (Calif.)—Fiction
 Mexican Americans—Fiction
 Moving, Household—Fiction
 Mystery and detective stories
 Single-parent families—Fiction
▶ **Setting:** Los Angeles, California
▶ **Interest Level:** age 11 & up
▶ **Reviewed:** *Booklist, Publishers Weekly, VOYA*

Sweet Fifteen

▶ **Author:** Diane Gonzales Bertrand
▶ **Publication:** Houston, TX: Pinata Books, 1995
▶ **LC#:** 94032656

▶ **Editions:**
 1558851224 hc.
 155885133X pb.
 0613179803 lib. bdg. Econo-Clad
▶ **Description:** 296 pages, 23 cm. Cover illustration by Gladys Ramírez.
▶ **Chapters:** 20
▶ **Summary:** When seamstress Rita Navarro makes a quinceañera dress for fourteen-year-old Stefanie, she finds herself becoming involved with the girl's family and attracted to her uncle.
▶ **Subjects:**
 Family life—Fiction
 Friendship—Fiction
 Mexican Americans—Fiction
 Quinceañera (Social custom)—Fiction
▶ **Interest Level:** ages 11–15, 13 & up, grades 8–12, 9–12, young adult
▶ **Reading Level:** 5.4
▶ **Tests:** Accelerated Reader
▶ **Reviewed:** *Booklist, Horn Book*
▶ **Awards:** Américas commended 1995, Tomás Rivera nominee 1995
▶ **Lists:** ALA Popular Paperbacks for Young Adults

Taking Sides

▶ **Author:** Gary Soto
▶ **Publication:** San Diego: Harcourt Brace Jovanovich, 1991
▶ **LC#:** 91011082
▶ **Editions:**
 0152840761 hc.
 015284077X pb. reprint
 078570499X lib. bdg. Econo-Clad

0613060563 lib. bdg. Econo Clad Spanish edition *Tomando Partido*
0788735160 audio tape, abridged Recorded Books
▶ **Description:** 138 pages, 22 cm. Cover illustration by Alan Mazzetti.
▶ **Chapters:** 13
▶ **Summary:** Fourteen-year-old Lincoln Mendoza, an aspiring basketball player, must come to terms with his divided loyalties when he moves from the Hispanic inner city to a white suburban neighborhood.
▶ **Subjects:**
Basketball—Fiction
Hispanic Americans—Fiction
Schools—Fiction
Single-parent families—Fiction
▶ **Setting:** San Francisco, California
▶ **Interest Level:** ages 9–12
▶ **Reading Level:** 4.4, 5.7
▶ **Tests:** Accelerated Reader, Reading Counts
▶ **Reviewed:** *Horn Book, Kirkus, School Library Journal, VOYA*
▶ **Lists:** New York Public Library's Books for the Teen Age
▶ **Web sites:** <www.jordan.palo-alto.ca.us/arcy/100/books/b0015.html>
[book discussion forum which allows one to make comments]

Thunder on the Sierra

▶ **Author:** Kathy Balmes
▶ **Publication:** New York: Silver Moon Press, 2001
▶ **LC#:** 00047023
▶ **Editions:**
1893110109 hc.
▶ **Description:** 89 pages, maps, 24 cm. Illustrated by Vicki Catapano.
▶ **Chapters:** 9
▶ **Summary:** In 1852, recently orphaned, thirteen-year-old Mateo becomes an "arreiro," or mule driver, bringing supplies to California gold miners and searching for the notorious bandit who stole his horse. When he learns that Yankee squatters are threatening to take the ranch he grew up on, Mateo heads for home.
▶ **Subjects:**
California—Fiction
Frontier and pioneer life—California—Fiction/Juvenile fiction
Gold mines and mining—California—Fiction
Mexican Americans—Fiction
Mules—Fiction
Orphans—Fiction
Robbers and outlaws—Fiction
▶ **Series:** Adventures in America
▶ **Interest Level:** ages 9–12, grades 3–6
▶ **Reviewed:** *School Library Journal*
▶ **Web site:**
<www.silvermoonpress.com/assets/PDFs/Arriero1-5.pdf>
▶ **Note:** Includes a chronology.
▶ **Note:** Historical fiction based loosely on the life of Ignacio Villegas who wrote *Boyhood Days Reminiscences of California in the*

1850's (San Francisco: California Historical Society, 1983)

▶ **Note:** Includes bibliographical references.

Trino's Choice

▶ **Author:** Diane Gonzales Bertrand
▶ **Publication:** Houston, TX: Piñata Books, 1999
▶ **LC#:** 98056132
▶ **Editions:**
1558852794 hc.
1558852689 pb.
▶ **Description:** 124 pages, 22 cm.
▶ **Chapters:** 14
▶ **Summary:** Frustrated by his poor financial situation and hoping to impress a smart girl, seventh-grader Trino falls in with a bad crowd led by an older teen with a vicious streak.
▶ **Subjects:**
Crime—Fiction
Mexican Americans—Fiction
▶ **Interest Level:** ages 9–12
▶ **Reading Level:** 4.9, 5.1
▶ **Tests:** Accelerated Reader, Reading Counts
▶ **Reviewed:** *Booklist*, *VOYA*
▶ **Awards:** Teddy Award winner (Austin Writers' League), Best Young Adult Book of the Year (*Fore Word* Magazine), Best Young Adult Fiction in English (Latino Literary Hall of Fame), Tomás Rivera Award nominee 1999
▶ **Lists:** Texas Lone Star 2001–2002

Trino's Time

▶ **Author:** Diane Gonzales Bertrand
▶ **Publication:** Houston, TX: Piñata Books, 2001
▶ **LC#:** 00065257
▶ **Editions:**
1558853162 hc.
1558853170 pb.
▶ **Description:** 171 pages, 22 cm.
▶ **Chapters:** 13 + epilogue
▶ **Summary:** With the help of some friends and a Tejano hero that he discovers in history class, thirteen-year-old Trino copes with his problems and his world.
▶ **Subjects:**
Mexican Americans—Fiction
▶ **Interest Level:** ages 9–12
▶ **Tests:** Reading Counts
▶ **Reviewed:** *VOYA*
▶ **Lists:** ALA Popular Paperbacks for Young Adults nominee 2002
▶ **Note:** Sequel to *Trino's Choice*

Two Worlds

- **Author:** Marietta Barrón
- **Publication:** Unionville, NY: Royal Fireworks Press, 1999
- **LC#:** 00504331
- **Editions:**
  088092120X pb.
- **Description:** 94 pages, 22 cm. Cover illustration by Chris Dodge.
- **Chapters:** 15
- **Summary:** Eleven-year-old José García plays baseball, defies segregation of the schools, wins a spelling bee, makes friends with an Anglo boy, runs away from home, and helps solve a family mystery in the small mining town of Aztec in 1926.
- **Subjects:**
  Baseball—Fiction
  Mexican Americans—Fiction
  Mexican Americans—Juvenile fiction
  Prejudices—Fiction
  Race relations—Fiction
- **Setting:** Southwestern U.S. mining town
- **Interest Level:** young adult

White Bread Competition

- **Author:** Jo Ann Yolanda Hernández
- **Publication:** Houston, TX: Piñata Books, 1997
- **LC#:** 97022159
- **Editions:**
  1558852107 pb.
  0613179811 lib. bdg. Econo-Clad
- **Description:** 208 pages, 22 cm. Cover illustration by Gladys Ramírez.

- **Chapters:** 10
- **Summary:** When Luz, a ninth-grade Latina student in San Antonio, wins a spelling competition, her success triggers a variety of emotions among family, friends, and the broader community.
- **Subjects:**
  Competition (Psychology)—Fiction
  English language—Spelling—Fiction
  Mexican Americans—Fiction
  Mexican Americans—Juvenile fiction
- **Setting:** San Antonio, Texas
- **Interest Level:** grades 7–12, grade 8 & up, young adult
- **Reading Level:** 4.4
- **Tests:** Accelerated Reader
- **Reviewed:** *Booklist*, *The Book Report*, *Hungry Mind Review*, *Library Journal*
- **Awards:** Américas commended 1997, Tomás Rivera nominee 1997, Second place Chicano/Latino Literary Prize (University of California, Irvine)
- **Web site:** <www.bronzeword.com> [One may submit reviews or comments about the book]
- **Note:** Ten interconnected stories

Woman Soldier

La Soldadera

- **Author:** Irene Beltrán Hernández
- **Publication:** Waco, TX: Blue Rose Books,1998
- **LC#:** 99068877
- **Editions:**
  096768300 pb.

▶ **Description:** 227 pages, 20 cm. Cover illustration by Viola Delgado.

▶ **Chapters:** 12

▶ **Summary:** (from book) "Nico Lorenzo, 17, discovers that her high school R.O.T.C. offers her a way out of a life of poverty and enables her to shed her gang-girl image."

▶ **Subjects:**
AIDS—Fiction
Death—Fiction
Gangs—Fiction
Ghosts—Fiction
Grandparents—Fiction
High schools—Fiction
Mexican Americans—Fiction

▶ **Setting:** Dallas, Texas

▶ **Interest Level:** grades 7–9, young adult

▶ **Awards:** Texas Institute of Letters, Finalist Best Book for Children or Young People 2001

Chapter 3

Latino Short Stories

The books included in this chapter are collections of contemporary short stories about modern-day children and teens written by a single author. Stories based on myths and legends are included in the folklore section, which follows. Biographical information on the short story authors in this chapter is included in Chapter 9, and a list of recognized Latino short story writers who have written for adult or general audiences is located in Chapter 10. A bibliography of Latino-authored anthologies is included at the end of the poetry and anthologies chapter.

Hopefully, librarians can use this listing of short stories to add diversity to short story collections in libraries. Educators can integrate these short stories into units on short stories and American literature and can use them as supplemental reading in many subject areas. Parents and students may find these short stories a useful starting point for sampling Latino literature and becoming acquainted with Latino writers.

Baseball in April and Other Stories

Béisbol en abril y otras historias

- ▶ **Author:** Gary Soto
- ▶ **Publication:** San Diego: Harcourt Brace Jovanovich, 1990, 2000 (English)
  Fondo de Cultura Economica, 1995 (Spanish)
  Holt, Rinehart, and Winston, 1998 (Spanish)
- ▶ **LC#s:**
  99057747
  91002426
  89036460
  00273727 (Spanish)
- ▶ **Editions:**
  0152025731 hc. 10th ed.
  0152025677 pb. 10th ed.
  015205720X hc
  0833574000 lib. bdg. Econo-Clad (English)
  1883332419 audiocassette, unabridged, Audio Bookshelf
  9681638549 pb. Fondo (Spanish)
  9681648382 pb.
  0613099877 lib. bdg. Econo-Clad (Spanish)
- ▶ **Description:** 111 pages, 20 cm.
- ▶ **Summary:** A collection of eleven short stories focusing on the everyday adventures of Hispanic young people growing up in Fresno, California.
- ▶ **Subjects:**
  Children's stories, American
  Mexican Americans—California—Fiction/Juvenile fiction
  Short stories
  Spanish language materials [Spanish version]
- ▶ **Interest Level:** ages 8–12, 9–12, grades 5–6, 5–9, young adult
- ▶ **Reading Level:** 5.1, 5.8
- ▶ **Tests:** Accelerated Reader, Reading Counts
- ▶ **Reviewed:** *Booklist, Horn Book, School Library Journal, VOYA*
- ▶ **Awards:** Pura Belpré Honor Book 1996
- ▶ **Lists:** ALA Best Books for Young Adults, *Booklist* Editor's Choice, *Horn Book* Fanfare, Indiana Practitioners' List
- ▶ **Web sites:**
  <www.sdcoe.k12.ca.us/score/soto/sototg.html>
  <http://ucsub.colorado.edu/~vallee/reading_lesson.htm>
  <http://134.126.10.30/~ramseyil/soto.htm>

El Bronx Remembered: A Novella and Stories

- ▶ **Author:** Nicholasa Mohr
- ▶ **Publication:** New York: Harper & Row, 1975
- ▶ **LC#s:**
  75006306
  8108658
- ▶ **Editions:**
  0064471004 pb. Harper
  087766779X hc. Peter Smith Pub.
  0613184432 lib. bdg. Econo-Clad
- ▶ **Description:** 263 pages, 18 cm.
- ▶ **Summary:** Twelve stories about growing up Puerto Rican in the South Bronx.
- ▶ **Subjects:**
  Bronx (New York, N.Y.)—Fiction
  Puerto Ricans—Fiction
- ▶ **Setting:** 1946–1956, after World War II
- ▶ **Interest Level:** age 12 & up, grades 7–12, young adult
- ▶ **Reading Level:** 4.2, 6.9

- ▶ **Tests:** Accelerated Reader, Reading Counts
- ▶ **Reviewed:** *San Francisco Chronicle, New York Times Book Review, School Library Journal*
- ▶ **Awards:** National Book Award Finalist 1976, *New York Times* Outstanding Book of the Year Finalist
- ▶ **Lists:** Notable Children's Trade Books in the Field of Social Studies (NCSS-CBC)

Crazy Loco

- ▶ **Author:** David Rice
- ▶ **Publication:** New York: Dial Books for Young Readers, 2001
- ▶ **LC#:** 00059042
- ▶ **Editions:**
  0803725981 hc
- ▶ **Description:** 135 pages, 24 cm. Cover illustration by Christian Clayton.
- ▶ **Summary:** A collection of nine stories about Mexican-American kids growing up in the Rio Grande Valley of South Texas.
- ▶ **Contents:**
  Sugarcane Fire
  Her Other Son
  Valentine
  Papa Lalo
  Crazy Loco
  Proud to Be an American
  She Flies
  The California Cousins
  Last Mass

- ▶ **Subjects:**
  Children's stories, American
  Mexican Americans—Fiction
  Mexican Americans—Juvenile fiction
  Short stories
  Texas—Fiction
  Texas—Juvenile fiction
- ▶ **Interest Level:** age 12 & up, grades 7–12, 7 & up
- ▶ **Reviewed:** *Booklist, Horn Book, School Library Journal, Texas Books in Review*

Fitting In

- ▶ **Author:** Anilú Bernardo
- ▶ **Publication:** Houston, TX: Piñata Books, 1996
- ▶ **LC#:** 96015676
- ▶ **Editions:**
  1558851763 hc.
  1558851739 pb.
  061317965X lib. bdg. Econo-Clad
- ▶ **Description:** 200 pages, 22 cm. Cover illustration by Daniel Lechón.
- ▶ **Summary:** A collection of stories about young girls who, as Cuban immigrants to the United States, grow in confidence and spirit as they confront painful challenges, meeting them head-on.
- ▶ **Contents:**
  Grandma Was Never Young
  Hurricane Friends
  A Do-It-Yourself Project
  Multiple Choices
  American Girls
- ▶ **Subjects:**
  Children's stories, American

Cubans—United States—Fiction
Cubans—United States—Juvenile fiction
Emigration and immigration—Fiction
Short stories
- ▶ **Setting:** Florida
- ▶ **Interest Level:** ages 9–12, 11 & up, grades 6–8, young adult
- ▶ **Reading Level:** 4.2
- ▶ **Tests:** Accelerated Reader
- ▶ **Reviewed:** *Booklist, Kirkus, Publishers Weekly, School Library Journal*
- ▶ **Awards:** *Skipping Stones* Exceptional Multicultural Books 1997, Paterson Prize for Young Adult Literature, 1997
- ▶ **Lists:** Birmingham Reads List 2000, 7th grade

The Horned Toad

- ▶ **Author:** Gerald Haslam
- ▶ **Illustrator:** Garth Haslam
- ▶ **Publication:** Petaluma, CA: Illustrated Editions, February 1995
- ▶ **Description:** 24 pages, comic book format, color cover, black-and-white illustrations
- ▶ **Summary:** "When Spanish speaking great-grandmother comes to stay, a family has to make big adjustments. 'The Horned Toad' is the story of how the great-grandmother's presence draws the family together, as they learn to appreciate the cultural differences between them."
- ▶ **Subjects:**
  Death—Fiction
  Family life—Fiction
  Grandparents—Fiction
  Horned toads—Fiction
- ▶ **Web site:** <www.sonic.net/~comix/tpp/>

- ▶ **Note:** Includes a glossary.
- ▶ **Note:** Includes a page on Horned Lizards (Horned Toads): genus Phrynosoma.
- ▶ **Note:** Story was originally published in short story format in *New Arts Review*, January, 1983 and has been reprinted in numerous anthologies.
- ▶ **Note:** Available only from Thwack! Pow! Productions, PO Box 751060, Petaluma, CA 94975-1060. Discounts available for schools and businesses.

The Ice Dove and

Other Stories

- ▶ **Author:** Diane de Anda
- ▶ **Publication:** Houston, TX: Arte Público Press, 1997
- ▶ **LC#:** 96050200
- ▶ **Editions:**
  1558851895 pb.
  0613179684 lib. bdg. Econo-Clad
- ▶ **Description:** 64 pages, 22 cm. Illustrated by Bob Pharr.
- ▶ **Summary:** A collection of short stories in which Hispanic-American children discover for themselves how special they are.
- ▶ **Contents:**
  The Ice Dove
  Pinto
  Something Special
  The Christmas Spirit Tree
- ▶ **Subjects:**
  Children's stories, American
  Hispanic Americans—Fiction

Hispanic Americans—Juvenile fiction
Self-esteem—Fiction
Self-esteem—Juvenile fiction
Short stories
► **Interest Level:** ages 8–12, 9–12
► **Reading Level:** 5.3
► **Tests:** Accelerated Reader
► **Reviewed:** *Booklist*
► **Awards:** Tomás Rivera nominee 1997
► **Note:** Spanish words are footnoted with English translations.

The Immortal Rooster
and Other Stories

► **Author:** Diane de Anda
► **Publication:** Houston, TX: Piñata Books, 1999
► **LC#:** 99010498
► **Editions:**
1558852786 pb.
► **Description:** 67 pages, 22 cm. Illustrated by Roberta Collier-Morales.
► **Summary:** A collection of stories that reflect the joys and disappointments of a variety of young Mexican Americans.
► **Contents:**
The Immortal Rooster
Dancing Miranda
Tía Luisa
Mari, Mari, Mariposa
The Visitors
► **Subjects:**
Children's stories, American
Hispanic Americans—Fiction
Hispanic Americans—Juvenile fiction
Short Stories

► **Interest Level:** ages 9–12
► **Note:** The story *Dancing Miranda* is now a picture book (Piñata Books, 2001).

In Nueva York

► **Author:** Nicholasa Mohr
► **Publication:** New York: Dial Press, 1977
Houston, TX: Arte Público Press, 1988
► **LC#:**
76042931 Dial
87018745 Arte
► **Editions:**
0934770786 pb. Arte
► **Description:** 193 pages, 22 cm. Cover illustration by Mark Piñón.
► **Summary:** Stories of New York's Puerto Rican neighborhood.
► **Contents:**
Old Mary
I Never Even Seen My Father
The English Lesson
The Perfect Little Flower Girl
The Operation
Lali
The Robbery
Coming to Terms
► **Subjects:**
Lower East Side (New York, N.Y.)—Fiction
New York (N.Y.)—Fiction
Puerto Ricans—Fiction

- ▶ **Interest Level:** young adult
- ▶ **Reviewed:** *Chicago Tribune, Los Angeles Times, New York Times, School Library Journal*
- ▶ **Lists:** *School Library Journal* Best Books for Young Adults

An Island Like You:

Stories of the Barrio

Una isla como tu

- ▶ **Author:** Judith Ortiz Cofer
- ▶ **Publication:** New York: Orchard Books, 1995
- ▶ **New York:** Puffin Books, 1996
  Fondo de Cultura Economica, 1999
- ▶ **LC#:**
  94032496 Orchard
  96023203 Puffin
- ▶ **Editions:**
  014038068X pb. Puffin
  0531087476 lib. bdg. Orchard
  0844669679 hc. Peter Smith Pub.
  0613015835 lib. bdg. Econo-Clad
  0613052447 lib. bdg. Econo-Clad (Spanish)
  9681654412 pb. Fondo (Spanish)
- ▶ **Description:** 165 pages, 19 cm. Cover illustration by Raul Colón.
- ▶ **Summary:** Twelve stories about young people caught between their Puerto Rican heritage and their American surroundings.
- ▶ **Subjects:**
  Children's stories, American
  Puerto Ricans—United States—Fiction
  Puerto Ricans—United States—Juvenile fiction
  Short stories

- ▶ **Interest Level:** grades 7–12, young adult
- ▶ **Reading Level:** 5.4, 7.1
- ▶ **Tests:** Accelerated Reader, Reading Counts
- ▶ **Reviewed:** *Booklist, Horn Book, Publishers Weekly, School Library Journal*
- ▶ **Awards:** Pura Belpré winner for narrative 1996
- ▶ **Lists:** ALA Best Books for Young Adults, ALA Popular Paperbacks for Young Adults, ALA Quick Picks for Reluctant Young Adult Readers
- ▶ **Setting:** Paterson, New Jersey
- ▶ **Web sites:**
  teachers
  <http://faculty.ssu.edu/~elbond/island.htm>
  <http://phoenix.liunet.edu/~dmutnick/wassign.html>
  students
  <http://www.rst2.edu/masters1999/BookClub/Island.htm>

Local News

- ▶ **Author:** Gary Soto
- ▶ **Publication:** San Diego: Harcourt Brace Jovanovich, 1993
- ▶ **LC#:** 92037905
- ▶ **Editions:**
  0152481176 hc.
  056048446X pb. Point
  0785736662 lib. bdg. Econo-Clad
- ▶ **Description:** 148 pages, 22 cm. Cover illustration by Francisco Mora.
- ▶ **Summary:** A collection of thirteen short stories about the everyday lives of Mexican-American young people in California's Central Valley.

► **Contents:**
Blackmail
Trick-or-Treating
First Job
Push-up
The School Play
The Raiders Jacket
The Challenge
Nacho Loco
The Squirrels
The Mechanical Mind
Nickel-a-Pound Plane Ride
New Year's Eve
► **Subjects:**
Children's stories, American
Mexican Americans—California—Fiction
Short stories
► **Interest Level:** grades 3–7, young adult
► **Reading Level:** 5.1, 5.9
► **Tests:** Accelerated Reader, Reading Counts
► **Reviewed:** *Horn Book, Kirkus*
► **Note:** Includes a glossary of Spanish words and phrases.

El Milagro and
Other Stories

► **Author:** Patricia Preciado Martin
► **Publication:** Tucson: The University of Arizona Press, 1996
► **LC#:** 95032550
► **Editions:**
0816515476 hc.
0816515484 pb.
► **Description:** 93 pages, 22 cm.

► **Contents:**
El Milagro = The Miracle
Dichos = Proverbs
La Toreadora = The Bullfighter
Bordados = Embroidery
Paraíso = Paradise
Orgullo = Pride
La Bendición = The Blessing
Reinas = Queens
La Bailarina = The Dancer
La Tortillera = The Tortilla Maker
Plumas = Feathers
La Virgen de la Soledad = The Virgin of Loneliness
La Creciente = The Flood
► **Subjects:**
Arizona—Social life and customs—Fiction
Mexican American women—Arizona—Social life and customs—Fiction
Mexican Americans—Arizona—Social life and customs—Fiction
► **Reviewed:** *Publishers Weekly*
► **Note:** Stories are in English. Spanish words and phrases are defined in footnotes.

Orange Candy Slices
and Other Secret Tales

► **Author:** Viola Canales
► **Publication:** Houston, TX: Piñata Books, 2001
► **LC#:** 2001032872
► **Editions:**
1558853324 pb.
► **Description:** 127 pages, 22 cm. Cover digital illustration by Giovanni Mora.

▶ **Contents:**
Orange Candy Slices
The Virgin
The Magi
The Carousel
Nopalitos
The Tiny Bubble
The Egg
The Feather
The Bubble Gum Pink House
The Polka Dot Dress
The Wooden Saints
The Flamingos
The Café
The magdalenas
The Woman with the Green Hair
The Tortilla
The panadería
The Magician
The Gold Clock
The Wooden Chair

▶ **Subjects:**
Girls—Fiction
Grandmothers—Fiction
Mexican-American families—Fiction

▶ **Setting:** South Texas

▶ **Interest Level:** young adult

Petty Crimes

▶ **Author:** Gary Soto
▶ **Publication:** San Diego: Harcourt Brace, 1998
▶ **LC#:** 97037114
▶ **Editions:**
0512016589 hc.
▶ **Description:** 157 pages, 22 cm. Cover illustration by Wayne Healy.

▶ **Summary:** A collection of short stories about Mexican-American youth growing up in California's Central Valley.

▶ **Contents:**
La Güera
Mother's Clothes
Try to Remember
The Boxing Lesson
Your Turn
Norma
The Funeral Suits
Little Scams
If the Shoe Fits
Frankie the Rooster
Born Worker

▶ **Subjects:**
Children's stories, American
Mexican Americans—California—Fiction
Mexican Americans—California—Juvenile fiction

▶ **Setting:** California

▶ **Interest Level:** ages 9–12, 12–15, grades 5–8, 5 & up

▶ **Reading Level:** 5

▶ **Tests:** Accelerated Reader

▶ **Reviewed:** *Booklist, Kirkus, Publishers Weekly, San Francisco Chronicle, School Library Journal*

▶ **Awards:** Américas commended 1998, Tomás Rivera nominee 1998

▶ **Lists:** ALA Quick Picks for Reluctant Young Adult Readers

Salsa Stories

▶ **Author:** Lulu Delacre

▶ **Publication:** New York: Scholastic Press, 2000

▶ **LC#:** 99025534

▶ **Editions:**
0590631187 hc.

▶ **Description:** 105 pages. 24 cm. Illustrated by Lulu Delacre.

▶ **Summary:** A collection of stories within the story of a family celebration where the guests relate their memories of growing up in various Latin-American countries. Also contains recipes.

▶ **Subjects:**
Latin America—Fiction

▶ **Interest Level:** ages 9–12, grades 3–7

▶ **Reading Level:** 4, 5.9

▶ **Reviewed:** *Booklist, Kirkus, Publishers Weekly, School Library Journal, VOYA*

▶ **Awards:** Américas commended 2000

▶ **Note:** Includes a glossary.

The Year of Our Revolution: New and Selected Stories and Poems

▶ **Author:** Judith Ortiz Cofer

▶ **Publication:** Houston, TX: Piñata Books, 1998

▶ **LC#:** 98013097

▶ **Editions:**
1558852247 hc.
141309741 pb. Puffin

▶ **Description:** 101 pages, 23 cm. Cover illustration by James F. Brisson.

▶ **Summary:** A collection of poems, short stories, and essays address the theme of straddling two cultures as do the offspring of Hispanic parents living in the United States.

▶ **Contents:**
Origin
Volar
The Meaning of El Amor
Vida
Fulana
Kennedy in the Barrio
Lost Relatives
Gravity
They Say Mamacita
First Love
Making Love in Spanish, circa 1969
The Year of Our Revolution
María Sabida
So Much for Mañana
El Olvido

▶ **Subjects:**
Hispanic Americans—Literary collections

▶ **Interest Level:** ages 9–12, grades 9–12

▶ **Reviewed:** *Booklist, Horn Book*

Chapter 4

Latino Folklore

This chapter contains collections of traditional short stories and folktales (cuentos) that have been handed down for generations. These titles represent Mexican-American, Puerto Rican, and Cuban-American traditions. Individual Latino folktales may have origins from a number of regions, including Mexico, Central America, South America, and Spain. Numerous Indian legends and folktales have been integrated into the cultural traditions of Latino groups; therefore, these collections also contain tales of the Taino, Zapotec, Muisca, Quecha, Chol, Aztecs, Maya, and U.S. Native Americans.

In this chapter, librarians will find Latino-specific titles to supplement library offerings, and teachers will find titles for use in language arts, speech, and Spanish classes as well as possible curriculum connections to history, geography, and home economics.

A list of professional storytellers is provided for those who may wish to contact a storyteller for school or community programs. Some storytellers visit schools, libraries, festivals, and conferences and do their storytelling in person, and several Latino storytellers have made folktales available in print and through recordings. Certainly, there may be other storytellers who are not known to the author, so searchers may discover other Latino storytellers. Additionally, this chapter includes a list of audiocassettes and compact discs by Latino storytellers.

Hopefully, parents will be able to locate appropriate books and cassettes to share with their children and to enjoy themselves. Students may wish to learn more about cultures by reading or listening to folktales. Folklore-based picture books by Latinos are not included in this guide.

Between Midnight and Morning: Historic Hauntings and Ghost Tales from the Frontier, Hispanic, and Native American Traditions

▶ **Author:** Patrick M. Mendoza
▶ **Publication:** Little Rock: August House Publishers, 2000
▶ **LC#:** 00056603
▶ **Editions:**
0874836077 pb.
▶ **Description:** 128 pages. 22 cm. Illustrated by Byron Taylor.
▶ **Contents:**
Old Jake and the Tlingit Rattle
The Skin Walker
The Ghosts of the Little Big Horn
The Night of Water
Hu-Waa-ka's Rifle
No Footprints in the Snow
The Return of Little Crow
Deer Woman
The Girl on Old Platte Road
The Ghost of Wounded Knee
El Chupacabras (The Cattle Eater)
No Goodbyes
The Moonlight Rider of Wyoming
The River of Lost Souls
The Hauntings of the Sheridan Inn
▶ **Subjects:**
Ghosts
Ghosts—West (United States)—Juvenile literature

▶ **Interest Level:** grades 4–6, young adult
▶ **Reviewed:** *Midwest Book Review, School Library Journal*
▶ **Note:** Includes a glossary.

The Corn Woman: Stories and Legends of the Hispanic Southwest

La Mujer del Maíz: Cuentos y Leyendas del Sudoeste Hispano

▶ **Author:** retold by Angel Vigil
▶ **Publication:** Englewood, CO: Libraries Unlimited Inc., 1994. Translated by Jennifer Audrey Lowell and Juan Francisco Marin.
▶ **LC#:** 94002091
▶ **Editions:**
1563081946 hc.
1563083949 audio cassette (English)
1563083957 audio cassette (Spanish)
▶ **Description:** 265 pages, 26 cm.
▶ **Contents:** Contains 45 cuentos in three sections:
In the Beginning: Stories from the Spirit of the Aztecs
The Aztec Creation Legend
Stories from the Merging of Two Cultures
The Traditional Cuentos
Moral and Religious Stories
Los Dos Compadres Stories
Chistes
Tales of Transformation, Magic, and Wisdom
Animal Stories

Contemporary Cuentos
Stories by Modern Latino Storytellers
▶ **Subjects:**
Hispanic Americans—Folklore
Indians of North America—Southwest,
New—Legends
Southwest, New—Folklore
▶ **Reviewed:** Book News, Inc.
▶ **Note:** Preface and introduction provide an excellent discussion of the origins and development of folklore.
▶ **Note:** Includes glossary and bibliography.

La Cuentista: Traditional Tales in Spanish and English

Cuentos tradicionales en español e ingles

▶ **Author:** Teresa Pijoan
▶ **Publication:** Santa Fe, NM: Red Crane Books, 1994
▶ **LC#:** 93038779
▶ **Editions:**
1878610430 hc.
1878610422 pb.
▶ **Description:** 206 pages, 23 cm. Illustrated by Rachel Lazo (text) and Alexandria Levin (cover). Translated by Nancy Zimmerman.
▶ **Contents:** Twenty-eight bilingual stories
▶ **Subjects:**
Hispanic Americans—Fiction
New Mexico—Social life and customs—Fiction
▶ **Interest Level:** young adult
▶ **Reviewed:** *Los Angeles Times*

▶ **Note:** Stories are in English and Spanish on facing pages.
▶ **Note:** Story notes in English and Spanish provide background for stories.

Dictionary of Chicano Folklore

▶ **Author:** Rafaela G. Castro
▶ **Publication:** Santa Barbara, CA: ABC-CLIO, 2000
▶ **LC#:** 00022477
▶ **Editions:**
0874369533 hc.
▶ **Description:** 349 pages. 27 cm. Illustrated with photographs. Cover illustration by Tony Ortega.
▶ **Subjects:**
Mexican Americans—Folklore—Dictionaries
Mexican Americans—Social life and customs—Dictionaries
▶ **Interest Level:** young adult, adult
▶ **Reviewed:** *The Book Report, Booklist*
▶ **Note:** Includes a bibliography and index.

The Eagle and the Rainbow: Timeless Tales from México

▶ **Author:** Antonio Hernández Madrigal
▶ **Publication:** Golden, CO: Fulcrum Kids, 1997
▶ **LC#:** 96046159
▶ **Editions:**
  1555913172 hc.
▶ **Description:** 57 pages. 24 cm. Illustrated by Tomie de Paola.
▶ **Contents:**
  The Eagle and the Rainbow: A Huichol Legend
  Tahui: A Tarahumara Legend
  The Boy Who Cried Tears of Jade: A Mayan Legend
  Tribe of the Deer: A Tarascan Legend
  Legend of the Feathered Serpent: An Aztec Legend
▶ **Subjects:**
  Folklore—Mexico
  Indians of Mexico—Folklore
▶ **Interest Level:** ages 9–12, grades 4–7
▶ **Reviewed:** *Booklist, Horn Book*
▶ **Note:** Includes a glossary.
▶ **Note:** Information sections after each story provide geographical and historical information about the people represented in the stories.

The Eagle on the Cactus: Traditional Stories from Mexico

El Águila encima del nopal: Cuentos Tradicionales de Mexico

▶ **Author:** retold by Angel Vigil
▶ **Publication:** Englewood, CO: Libraries Unlimited, Inc., 2000
▶ **LC#:** 00027130
▶ **Editions:**
  1563087030 hc.
▶ **Description:** 223 pages. 27 cm. Illustrated with black-and-white sketches and color plates. Translated by Francisco Miraval
▶ **Contents:**
  Essential Legends
  Creation Stories from Indigenous Mexico
  Stories from Spanish Colonial Mexico
▶ **Subjects:**
  Indians of Mexico—Folklore
  Indians of Mexico—Social life and customs
  Legends—Mexico
  Tales—Mexico
▶ **Series:** World Folklore series
▶ **Note:** Includes glossary of Spanish words, suggested readings, index, and author's biography.
▶ **Note:** 45 stories in English and Spanish.

Golden Tales: Myths, Legends, and Folktales from Latin America

De oro y esmeraldas: mitos, leyendas y cuentos popules de latinoamérica

- ▶ **Author:** Lulu Delacre
- ▶ **Publication:** New York: Scholastic, 1996 (English), 1998 (Spanish), 2001
- ▶ **LC#:** 94036724
- ▶ **Editions:**
  0590481878 pb. (English)
  059048186X hc. (English)
  043924398X pb. reprint (English)
  059048186X hc. (English)
  0613357213 lib. bdg. Econo-Clad (English)
  0590676849 pb. (Spanish)
  0613107012 lib. bdg. Econo-Clad (Spanish)
- ▶ **Description:** 74 pages, 78 pages. 29 cm. illustrations, maps. Illustrated by Lulu Delacre.
- ▶ **Contents:** Twelve stories from thirteen countries including Mexico, Puerto Rico, Colombia, and others. Stories of four native cultures: Taino, Zapotec, Muisca, and Quechua.
- ▶ **Subjects:**
  Indian mythology—Latin America
  Indians—Folklore
  Legends—Latin America
  Tales—Latin America
  Spanish language materials
- ▶ **Interest Level:** ages 4–8, 8 & up, grades 3–7, 4–6
- ▶ **Reading Level:** 4, 6.3, 6.8
- ▶ **Tests:** Reading Counts (English)

Accelerated Reader (Spanish)
- ▶ **Reviewed:** *Booklist, Kirkus, Publishers Weekly, School Library Journal*
- ▶ **Note:** Includes bibliographical references.
- ▶ **Note:** Includes pronunciation guide for Indian and Spanish words.

Listen, a Story Comes: Bilingual Stories in Spanish and English

Escucha, que viene un cuento

- ▶ **Author:** Teresa Pijoan
- ▶ **Publication:** Santa Fe, NM: Red Crane Books, 1996
- ▶ **LC#:** 96033039
- ▶ **Editions:**
  1878610597 pb.
- ▶ **Description:** ix, 203 pages, 23 cm. Illustrated by Gary Bigelow. Translated by Sharon Franco.
- ▶ **Subjects:**
  Hispanic Americans—Fiction
  New Mexico—Fiction
- ▶ **Interest Level:** young adult

Mexican Ghost Tales of the Southwest

- ▶ **Authors:** Alfred Avila and Kat Avila
- ▶ **Publication:** Houston, TX: Piñata Books, 1994
- ▶ **LC#:** 94006919
- ▶ **Editions:**
  1558851070 pb.
  0785754881 lib. bdg. Econo-Clad
- ▶ **Description:** 172 pages. 22 cm. Illustrated by Alfred Avila.
- ▶ **Contents:** Twenty-one stories:
  La Llorona
  The Devil Dog
  The Bad Boy
  The Witches
  The Pepper Tree
  The Devil and the Match
  The Devil Baby
  The Devil's Wind
  The Funeral and the Goat Devil
  The Dead Man's Shoes
  The Yaqui Indian and the Dogs
  The Caves of Death
  The Acorn Tree Grove
  The Water Curse
  The Bat
  The Japanese Woman
  The Brutish Indian
  The Whirlwind
  The Chinese Woman of the Sea
  La Llorona of the Moon
  The Owl
- ▶ **Subjects:**
  Ghost stories
  Mexican Americans—Folklore
  Tales—Southwest, New

- ▶ **Reviewed:** *Booklist*
- ▶ **Interest Level:** young adult

Magic Moments

Momentos mágicas

- ▶ **Author:** Olga Loya
- ▶ **Publication:** Little Rock, Ark: August House, 1997
- ▶ **LC#:** 97038582
- ▶ **Editions:**
  087483497X pb.
  0613262506 lib. bdg. Econo-Clad
- ▶ **Description:** 188 pages, illustrated, 22 cm. Translated by Carmen Lizardi-Rivera
- ▶ **Contents:** Four sections:
  Scary Stories
  Trickster Tales
  Strong Women
  Myths
- ▶ **Subjects:**
  Spanish-language materials—Bilingual
  Tales—Latin America
- ▶ **Interest Level:** ages 9–12, grades 3–7, 4–8
- ▶ **Reading Level:** 5
- ▶ **Reviewed:** *Kirkus, School Library Journal*
- ▶ **Awards:** Aesop Accolade Award 1998, Américas Award commended 1998
- ▶ **Lists:** Young Adults' Choices, International Reading Association
- ▶ **Note:** Stories are from the Chol People, Mexico, Colombia, Cuba, Nicaragua, Puerto Rico, Guatemala, the Aztecs, and the Mayas.
- ▶ **Note:** Some stories available on audiotape *Tío Conejo (Uncle Rabbit) and Other Latin American Trickster Tales*, 0-87483-580-1,

46 minutes, read by Olga Loya.
► **Note:** In English and Spanish.
► **Note:** Includes bibliographical references.

My Land Sings: Stories from the Rio Grande

► **Author:** Rudolfo Anaya
► **Publication:** New York: Morrow Junior Books, 1999
► **LC#:** 99019040
► **Editions:**
0688150780 hc.
► **Description:** 176 pages, illustrated, 22 cm. Cover illustration by Amy Córdova.
► **Summary:** A collection of ten original and traditional stories set in New Mexico, including "Lupe and la Llorona," "The Shepherd Who Knew the Language of Animals," and "Coyote and Raven."
► **Contents:**
Lupe and la Llorona
Dulcinea
The Three Brothers
Doña Sebastiana
The Shepherd Who Knew the Language of Animals
The Fountain of Youth
The Lost Camel
The Miller's Good Luck
Sipa's Choice
Coyote and Raven
► **Subjects:**
Children's stories, American
Folklore—New Mexico
New Mexico—Fiction
New Mexico—Juvenile fiction
Short stories
Tales—New Mexico
► **Interest Level:** age 10 & up
► **Reading Level:** 6
► **Reviewed:** *Booklist, Kirkus, Publishers Weekly, School Library Journal*
► **Awards:** Tomás Rivera Award 1999

Señor Cat's Romance and Other Favorite Stories from Latin America

► **Author:** Lucia M. González
► **Publication:** New York: Scholastic, 1997, 2001
► **LC#:** 95034144
► **Editions:**
0439278635 pb. reprint
0613357493 lib. bdg. Econo-Clad
► **Description:** 48 pages, 26 cm. Illustrated by Lulu Delacre.
► **Summary:** A collection of popular tales told to young children in places such as Argentina, Cuba, Colombia, Nicaragua, and Mexico.
► **Contents:** six folktales
► **Subjects:**
Folklore
Latin Americans—Folklore
Tales—Latin America
► **Interest Level:** ages 4–8, baby-preschool, grades P–2, 1–3
► **Reading Level:** 1.5
► **Tests:** Reading Counts

- ▶ **Reviewed:** *Booklist, Horn Book, Publishers Weekly, School Library Journal*
- ▶ **Awards:** Américas commended title 1997.
- ▶ **Note:** Includes glossaries.
- ▶ **Note:** Notes at the end of each story give the origins and variants.

Spanish-American Folktales: The Practical Wisdom of Spanish-Americans in 28 Eloquent and Simple Stories

- ▶ **Author:** Teresa Pijoan de Van Etten
- ▶ **Publication:** Little Rock, Ark: August House, 1990
- ▶ **LC#:** 90042303
- ▶ **Editions:**
  0874831555
- ▶ **Description:** 127 pages, 17 x 25 cm. Illustrated by Wendell E. Hall.
- ▶ **Contents:**
  Leaf Monster
  Lizard
  The Shoes
  Magician Flea
  The Two Friends
  Witches
  River Man
  Chicken Dinner
  The Mare
  Owl Wishes
  Leticia's Turtle
  Wise Stone
  Meadowlark
  The Wooden Horse
  The River
  The Flea
  Remember
  The Prayer
  The Three Sisters and Luck
  The Sheepskin
  Postman
  Eyes That Come Out at Night
  The Mule
  The Ant
  The Animals' Escape
  The Dispute
  The Mountain Lion and the Mouse
  The Dead One Fell
- ▶ **Subjects:**
  Spanish Americans—New Mexico—Folklore
  Tales—New Mexico
- ▶ **Interest Level:** ages 9–12
- ▶ **Note:** Author discusses the importance, cultures, traditions, individuals, and stories.
- ▶ **Note:** In English only.
- ▶ **Note:** A section at the end explains "Where the Stories Came From."

Stories from a Dark and Evil World: Bilingual Tales

Cuentos del mundo malevolo

► **Author:** Teresa Pijoan
► **Publication:** Santa Fe, NM: Red Crane Books/Consortium Book Sales, 1999
► **LC#:** 99023217
► **Editions:**
  1878610716 pb.
► **Description:** 229 pages. 23 cm. Illustrated by Daniel Kosharek. Translated by Sharon Franco.
► **Contents:**
  The Dreaming Bachelor = El sueño del soltero
  The Heartsick Lover = Mal de amores
  The Gloves = Los guantes
  Blood Hungry = Ávido de sangre
  Master of Death = El maestro de la muerte
  Casino Night = Noche de casino
  The Lover's Mask = La máscara del amante
  Night Hag = La bruja de noche
  Dead Wife's Revenge = La venganza de la difunta esposa
  Gavin's Story = La historia de Gavin
  The Love of Gold = El amor al oro
  The Oscars = Los Óscares
  The Chile Plant = El mata de chile
► **Subjects:**
  Hispanic Americans—Fiction
  Horror tales, American—Translations into Spanish
  New Mexico—Fiction
► **Interest Level:** young adult

► **Reviewed:** *Multicultural Review, New Mexico Magazine*
► **Awards:** Latino Literary Hall of Fame 2000
► **Note:** English and Spanish on facing pages.

Multicultural Stories and Storytellers

Listed below are some professional storytellers with contact information and brief biographical sketches. This list represents persons who are actively involved in storytelling and are available for programs. Following this section is a list of audiotapes by Latino storytellers. Readers are encouraged to investigate these persons and materials to determine if they will meet individual needs and situations. Information is taken from storytellers, individual Web sites, and personal e-mail messages.

Paulette Atencio – Mexican American
Box 72, Chama, NM 87520, Telephone: 505-756-2207

Paulette Atencio is a professional bilingual storyteller and author. She has experience working with all ages and is willing to travel across the country to provide performances and workshops. Her books include *Cuentos from Long Ago* and *Cuentos from My Childhood* from the Museum of New Mexico Press.

Elida Guardia Bonet – Puerto Rican
9801 Oxaus Lane, Austin, TX 78759, Telephone: 512-345-7608, Fax: 512-345-7610
e-mail: mangopit@storyteller.net, Web site: <www.underthemangotree.com>

Elida Bonet was born in Puerto Rico and grew up in Panama. She has taught social studies and Spanish at middle school and elementary levels. Bonet is available for storytelling and workshops for all ages. She provides stories of Latin America and special programs for Hispanic Heritage month, Día de la Raza, and other holidays.

Dianne de Las Casas – Multicultural
e-mail: dlcstory@bellsouth.net, Web site: <www.storyconnection.net>

Dianne de Las Casas' family represents a multicultural Latino mix. Her heritage is Filipino and Caucasian; she lived in Spain as a child, and her husband is of Cuban and Honduran descent. De Las Casas, who is active locally, regionally, and nationally, integrates Spanish into her programs.

Leeny Del Seamonds – Hispanic
Contact: Gail A. LaRocca, The LaRocca Agency, 7 Mt. Pleasant Street,
Winchester, MA 01890, Telephone: 781-729-1537, e-mail: GailALaRocca@cs.com

Leeny Del Seamonds is an actor, singer, mime, director, and performer. A professional development provider for the New Jersey and Massachusetts departments of education, she offers programs and workshops on folktales and original stories. Her offerings include storytelling, workshops, and residencies at museums, libraries, and schools.

Mary Ellen Gonzales – bicultural
2806 Calle Campeon, Santa Fe, NM 87505, Telephone: 505-438-6265
e-mail: storyteler@cybermesa.com, Web site: <www.nmeh.org>

Mary Ellen Gonzales is bicultural—half Spanish and half Anglo. She calls herself a "coyote" and considers building bridges between cultures a life task. Her specialty is Hispanic stories, but she tells stories from many cultures, including Native American. Having grown up in a ranching family on the New Mexico-Colorado border, Gonzales feels a connection to the land and is dedicated to promoting an understanding of cultural values through storytelling.

Patrick Mendoza – Cuban/Irish/Indian American
1566 Adams Street, Denver, CO 80206, Telephone: 303-388-8097
e-mail: patmendoza@aol.com, Web site: <www.users.aol.com/patmendoza/>

Pat Mendoza is a writer, musician, and storyteller. For more than 26 years, he has provided programs for a variety of audiences in nursing homes, prisons, and mental institutions as well as schools. A former police officer, he is comfortable working with special education and at-risk students and works with kindergarten through adult levels. A multilingual, multi-faceted performer and teacher, Mendoza offers teacher in-service training and residencies for history, language arts, writing, music, and speech/drama.

Gregorio Pedroza – Mexican American
4 Deborah Drive, Apalachin, NY 13732
e-mail: gpedroza@prodigy.net, Web site: <http://home.stny.rr.com/gpedroza>

Gregorio Pedroza is a bilingual storyteller, a motivational speaker, and a poet. He grew up in Texas and worked for IBM until retirement. A cancer survivor, Pedroza copes with chronic pain through storytelling and writing. He is available for workshops on writing and story-telling. His programs include interactive stories, myths and legends, tall tales, traditional sto-ries, and alliterative stories.

Antonio Rocha – Brazilian American
165 Brackett St. #1, Portland, ME 04102, Telephone: 207-771-5494
e-mail:rochact@maine.rr.com, Web site: <http://home.maine.rr.com/rocha>

Antonio Rocha of Twilight Productions is a native of Brazil. He came to the United States in 1988 after receiving a Partners of the Americas grant. A storyteller, actor, and mime, Rocha travels around the world, but Maine continues to be his home base.

Antonio Sacre – Cuban/Irish American
PO Box 3444, Hollywood, CA 90078-3444, Telephone: 888-654-6436
e-mail: asacre@earthlink.net, Web site: <www.antoniosacre.com>

Growing up as a "Latino in a white world and white in a Latino world," Antonio Sacre stopped speaking Spanish after he was teased in kindergarten but relearned Spanish years later. In his storytelling he tries to motivate children to learn English while preserving their cultural heritage. Seeking to encourage achievement, self-esteem, and cultural pride, he provides training for teachers and parents on the use of storytelling. His story *The Barking Mouse* is published in the Fall 2001 issue of *Teaching Tolerance* magazine and is available online at <www.tolerance.org/storybooks/mouse/index.html>.

Consuelo Samarripa – Mexican American
12335 Deerbrook Trail, Austin, TX 78750-1059, Telephone: 512-258-4021
e-mail: Csamarripa@storyteller.net
Web site: <www.members.aol.com/asconsuelo/Bilingual/Storyteller.html>

Samarripa is a second-generation Texas native from San Antonio. Her stories focus on history, heritage, poetry, and folklore.

Tió Alecc Seth Sherwood-Flores – Multicultural
PO Box 80878, Rancho Santa Margarita, CA 92688, Telephone: 949-888-7365
e-mail: tioalecc@msn.com, Web site: <www.storyteller.net/tellers/tioalecc/>

Tió Alecc is a high school English teacher who feels strongly about preserving the language and culture of his Guatemalan mother. He works with Mimi, the reading gorilla, and his assistant/daughter Melinda in a bilingual musical show they present at libraries, schools, conventions, and special events, primarily in California.

Audiocassettes and CDs by Latino Storytellers

Capirotada: Stories from my Barrio by Gregorio Pedroza. Firekeeper Publications. Stories of growing up in a Mexican-American barrio in South Texas. In English. Includes Sancho el Rey, La Llorona, The Rabbit in the Moon, El Chupacabras, and others.

Celebrating as Hard as We Work by Gregorio Pedroza. Firekeeper Publications. Four stories portraying the joys of religious and patriotic holidays, family values, and the reality of work and a work ethic told in a lively, humorous manner.

The Corn Woman: Audio Stories and Legends of the Hispanic Southwest by Angel Vigil. Libraries Unlimited, 1995. World Folklore Series. ISBN: 1563083965 English and Spanish. 1563083949 (English) ISBN: 1563083957 (Spanish). Nine selected stories from the book. Reviewed *School Library Journal.*

Debajo del árbol de mango: Cuentos de países de habla hispana by Elida Guardia Bonet. Zaratí Press, 1999. ISBN: 0966366212. Spanish version of *Under the Mango Tree*. A Spanish presentation of six stories, four folktales, and two original stories by Bonet. Parents' Choice Silver Award, 2000. Reviewed *Booklist.*

Growing Up Cuban in Decatur, Georgia by Carmen Agra Deedy. Peachtree Publishers, 1995. 156145161X. Twelve short stories originally broadcast on National Public Radio. Audiofile Earphones Award winner.

Lírica Infantil by José Luis Orozco. Arcoiris Records. 13-volume set includes cassettes, CDs, and songbooks. Vols. 1-3 Latin American Children's Songs, 4. Animales y Movimiento, 5. Letras, Numeros y Colores, 6. Fiestas/Holidays, 7. Navidad y Pancho Claus, 8. Arrullos: Lullabies in Spanish, 9. De Colores and Other Latin American Folk Songs for Children, 10. Corridos mexicanos y chicanos, 11. Esta es mi tierra/This Land is My Land, 12. Diez deditos, 13. Canto y Cuento. Some listed songbooks illustrated by Elisa Kleven and published by Dutton.

Looking for Papito: Family Stories from Latin America by Antonio Sacre. Woodside Avenue Music Productions, 1996. ISBN: 1886283095. American Story series. In English and Spanish. Parents' Choice Gold Award 1996, NAPPA Gold Award 1997

Rabbit Tales = Los cuentos de Tío Conejo by Elida Bonet. Zaratí Press, 2000. ISBN: 0966366220. Bilingual retelling of rabbit tales. Parents' Choice Silver Award, 2000.

Stories from the Heart/Cuentos con todo Corazon by Gregorio Pedroza. Firekeeper Publications. Four warm and humorous stories about Pedroza's boyhood in South Texas.

Tío Conejo (Uncle Rabbit) and Other Latin American Trickster Tales by Olga Loya. August House Audio, 1999. ISBN: 08744835801. Four stories in English and Spanish from *Momentos Mágicas/Magic Moments*.

Under the Mango Tree: Stories from Spanish Speaking Countries by Elida G. Bonet. Zaratí Press, 1998. ISBN: 0966366204. Four traditional Latin-American folktales and two original stories from Bonet's childhood in English with Spanish words and phrases.

Water Torture, the Barking Mouse and Other Tales of Wonder by Antonio Sacre. Woodside Avenue Music Productions, 2000. ISBN: 188628315X. Folktales from Mexico and legends of La Llorona and others. Parents' Choice Silver Honor Winner 2000.

Winsome Winona and Other Alliterative Stories by Gregorio Pedroza. Firekeeper Publications. Six stories in which each word begins with the same letter. English and Spanish with Spanish words translated.

Addresses

Arcoiris Records, PO Box 7428, Berkeley, CA 94707, Telephone: 888-354PEPE, Fax: 510-654-1469, Web site: <http://joseluisorozco.com/>

August House, PO Box 3223, Little Rock, AR 72203-3223, Telephone: 501-372-5450, Fax: 501-372-5579, Web site:

Firekeeper, 4 Deborah Drive, Apalachin, NY 13732, Web site: <http://home.stny.rr.com/gpedroza>

Libraries Unlimited, PO Box 6633, Englewood, CO 80155-6633, Web site: <www.lu.com/index.html>

Peachtree Publishers, 1700 Chattahoochee Avenue, Atlanta, GA 30318-2112, Telephone: 800-241-0113 (call direct for 20% discount on cassettes), Web site: <www.peachtreeonline.com/index.html>

Woodside Avenue Music Productions, 2859 Central Street #109, Evanston, IL 60201, Telephone: 800-594-9180, Web site: <www.woodsideavenue.com>

Zaratí Press, Elida Bonet, 9801 Oxaus Lane, Austin, TX 78759, Telephone: 512-345-7608, Fax: 512-345-7610, Web site: <www.underthemangotree.com>

Chapter 5

Latino Drama

Latino drama, a "cousin" of folklore, has a long history in the United States. Spanish missionaries and soldiers brought a tradition of religious and folk theater when they came to colonize. It is likely that the first drama on present-day U.S. soil was performed and witnessed by Juan de Oñate and his group in 1598 in New Mexico.

Religious and folk dramas combined with elements of Native-American ceremonies to produce plays for teaching and entertainment. In the days before movies, tent shows (carpas) were common across the Southwest. In the 1960s, Teatro Campesino began in the fields of California as a teaching tool used by Luis Valdez and César Chávez to educate workers and the public about the working conditions of migrant farm workers. Puerto Rican, Cuban, and Mexican-American theatrical traditions have combined to provide the Latino drama we enjoy today.

This chapter includes book-length plays, play scripts, and collections of plays. Librarians may wish to consider these titles for purchase to supplement the drama offerings of their libraries. Teachers should consider these plays for classroom reading, for public presentations, as a basis for comparison to other genres, and for supplemental reading and activities in language arts, speech, drama, history, and geography classes.

Students and parents may wish to read Latino-authored plays for pleasure and to learn. Chapter 10 includes a list of Latino dramatists for those wishing to learn more about Latino drama in general. All readers are reminded that payment of royalties is required for public performance of most of these plays. If in doubt, ask.

¡Aplauso! Hispanic Children's Theater

- **Editor:** Joe Rosenberg
- **Publication:** Houston, TX: Piñata Books, 1995
- **LC#:** 94036005
- **Editions:**
  1558851364 hc.
  1558851275 pb
- **Description:** 274 pages, 23 cm. Illustrated by Daniel Lechón.
- **Summary:** A collection of plays for children written by Hispanic-American authors.
  Plays in English:
  Fred Menchaca and Filemón by José G. Gaytán
  The Caravan by Alvan Colón
  Bocón by Lisa Loomer
  The Day They Stole All the Colors by Héctor Santiago
  The Legend of the Golden Coffee Bean by Manuel Martín, Jr.
  Bilingual Plays:
  El gato sin amigos = The Cat Who Had No Friends by Joe Rosenberg
  Song of the Oak = El canto del roble by Roy Conboy
  Plays in Spanish:
  Fred Menchaca y Filemón de José G. Gaytán
  La caravana de Alvan Colón
  El día que robaron los colores de Héctor Santiago
  La lente maravillosa de Emilio Carballido
- **Subjects:**
  Children's plays, American—Hispanic-American authors
  Hispanic Americans—Drama
  Hispanic Americans—Juvenile drama
  Plays—Hispanic American authors
- **Interest Level:** ages 4–8, all ages
- **Reviewed:** *Midwest Book Review*
- **Note:** Includes biographies and background information.

Four Play Scripts by Carlos Morton

- **Author:** Carlos Morton
- **Publication:** Studio City, CA: Players Press
  Players Press, PO Box 1132, Studio City, CA 91614-0132
- **Interest Level:** young adult

At Risk (A Learning Piece about AIDS)

- **LC#:** 97013870
- **Editions:**
  0887344429 pb.
- **Description:** 14 pages, one act, two scenes, copyright 1997
- **Summary:** Five Hispanic high school students learn a dramatic lesson about at-risk behavior and the AIDS virus.
- **Subjects:**
  AIDS (Disease)—Drama
  AIDS (Disease) in adolescence—Juvenile drama

Hispanic Americans—Drama
Plays
▶ **Note:** Characters are ages 15–17.
▶ **Note:** Available in Spanish

The Drop-Out

▶ **LC#:** 96039957
▶ **Editions:**
0887344437 pb.
▶ **Description:** 15 pages, one act, ten scenes, copyright 1997
▶ **Catalog Summary:** "Franky Medina wants to drop out of school because he doesn't get along with his English teacher. Franky's family is very poor and there is no father in the home. Franky believes he can help pay the bills by working full time . . . believes that he may have to assist his younger sister, Rosie, who at thirteen thinks she may be pregnant."
▶ **Subjects:**
Family problems—Drama
Mexican Americans—Drama
Plays
Young adult drama, American

Drug-O the Magnificent

▶ **LC#:** 96039709
▶ **Editions:**
0887344445 pb.
▶ **Description:** 18 pages, one act, copyright 1997

▶ **Summary:** Drug-O, a walking drug store, gleefully dispenses all varieties of drugs and delights in describing how he infiltrates every aspect of a family's life causing its destruction.
▶ **Subjects:**
Drug abuse—Drama
Drug abuse—Juvenile drama
Family problems—Drama
Plays
Problem families—Juvenile drama
Young adult drama, American

Los Fatherless

▶ **LC#:** 96039713
▶ **Editions:**
0887343767 pb.
▶ **Description:** 23 pages, one act, copyright 1997
▶ **Summary:** Following his stabbing by a member of a rival gang, Benito refuses to tell who did it, vowing instead to seek revenge "the barrio way."
▶ **Subjects:**
Gangs—Drama
Gangs—Texas—El Paso—Juvenile drama
Mexican-American youth—Texas—El Paso—Juvenile drama
Mexican Americans—Drama
Plays
Young adult drama, American

Nerdlandia: A Play

▶ **Author:** Gary Soto
▶ **Publication:** New York: PaperStar/Putnam, 1999
▶ **LC#:** 98037093
▶ **Editions:**
0698117840 pb.
▶ **Description:** 88 pages
▶ **Summary:** A humorous play in which Martin, a Chicano nerd, undergoes a transformation with the help of his friends and experiences true love.
▶ **Subjects:**
Mexican-American youth—Juvenile drama
Mexican Americans—Drama
Plays
Young adult drama, American
▶ **Interest Level:** ages 9–12, 12 & up, grades 7–12
▶ **Reading Level:** 6.8, 7
▶ **Tests:** Reading Counts
▶ **Reviewed:** *Booklist, Horn Book*
▶ **Characters:** Martin (nerdish boy), Joaquin (vato loco), Freddie and Tito (humorous vatos locos, Ceci (love-struck chola), Lupe and Susana (cholas)
▶ **Note:** Includes a glossary of Spanish words and phrases.

Novio Boy: A Play

▶ **Author:** Gary Soto
▶ **Publication:** San Diego, CA: Harcourt Brace, 1997
▶ **LC#:** 96032605
▶ **Editions:**
0152015310 pb.
0613022858 lib. bdg. Econo-Clad
▶ **Description:** 78 pages, 21 cm. Cover illustration by Amanda Schaffer.
▶ **Summary:** Rudy anxiously prepares for and then goes out on a first date with an attractive girl who is older than he is.
▶ **Subjects:**
Children's plays, American
Dating (Social customs)—Drama
Dating (Social customs)—Juvenile drama
Plays
Teenage boys—Juvenile drama
▶ **Setting:** Fresno, California
▶ **Characters:** Rudy (ninth grader), Alex (from *The Pool Party*), Patricia (eleventh grader), Alicia (eleventh grader), Rudy's Mother, Uncle Juan, El Gato (radio disc jockey), Mama Rosa (curandera of love), Estela, radio show callers, old man, waiter
▶ **Interest Level:** ages 7–12, 9–12, 12 & up, grades 6–8, young adult
▶ **Reading Level:** 5.7, 7
▶ **Tests:** Reading Counts
▶ **Reviewed:** *Booklist, School Library Journal*
▶ **Awards:** Américas commended 1997
▶ **Note:** Includes a glossary of Spanish words and phrases.
▶ **Note:** Contains seven scenes.

Teatro! Hispanic Plays

for Young People

- ▶ **Author:** Angel Vigil
- ▶ **Publication:** Englewood, CO: Teacher Ideas Press/Libraries Unlimited, 1996
- ▶ **LC#:** 96015593
- ▶ **Editions:**
  156308371X pb.
- ▶ **Description:** 186 pages, 28 cm. illustrated
- ▶ **Summary:** Consists of fourteen scripts for classroom use based upon Hispanic culture and traditions of the American Southwest.
- ▶ **Contents:**
  Part I Folktales
  The Three Pieces of Good Advice
  The Most Interesting Gift of All
  Blanca Flor = White Flower
  El Muchacho que Mato al Gigante = The Boy Who Killed the Giant
  Juan Oso = John the Bear
  La Estrella de Oro = The Gold Star
  Part II Animal Fables
  The Littlest Ant
  The Smelly Feet
  The Foolish Coyote
  Part III Holiday Plays
  El Día de Los Muertos = The Fiesta of the Day of the Dead
  La Aparición de Nuestra Señora de Guadalupe = The Miracle of Our Lady of Guadalupe
  La Flor de La Noche Buena = The Flower of the Holy Night
  Los Pastores = The Shepherds
  Part IV Historical Play
  La Batalla de Cinco de Mayo = The Battle of Cinco de Mayo

- ▶ **Subjects:**
  Children's plays, American
  Hispanic Americans—Drama
  Hispanic Americans—Juvenile drama
  Plays
- ▶ **Interest Level:** grades 3–9, 4–8, elementary and middle school
- ▶ **Reviewed:** *Booklist*
- ▶ **Note:** Includes bibliographical references, background information on each play, necessary props, lists of characters, staging tips, and costume sketches.

Three Plays in Two

Languages

Tres obras drammaticas en dos idiomas

- ▶ **Author:** Alice Morin
- ▶ **Publication:** Palm Springs, CA: Los Abuelos Press, 1997
- ▶ **LC#:** 99216309
- ▶ **Editions:**
  0965885410 pb.
- ▶ **Description:** 53 pages, 22 cm. Illustrated by Joel Morin. Translated by Irene Farber.
- ▶ **Interest Level:** grades 6–12

► **Contents:**

¡Esta Computadora no es Bilingue! This Computer Is Not Bilingual!

   Characters: Stanley (born in Pennsylvania), Fran (born in Oregon), Ileana (born in Mexicali), José (born in El Salvador)

   Setting: a secondary classroom with computers

   Playing time: approximately 20 minutes

Where Is the Border? ¿Dónde Está La Frontera?

   Characters: Juan (teen of Mexican ancestry), Lewis (teen of Irish ancestry), Henry (store owner from England), Señora Torres (teacher of mixed ancestry), Cissy (Lewis's sister)

   Setting: small town in the Southwest about 1840

¡Abuelo! ¡Abuelo! Grandpa! Grandpa!

   Characters: two teens, wife of Sancho, Sancho, Grandpa

   Setting: Southwestern United States, farm area

► **Subjects:**

Children's plays, American
Hispanic Americans—Juvenile drama
Languages in contact—Juvenile drama

► **Reviewed:** *NEA Journal*

► **Note:** Each play is one act.

► **Note:** English and Spanish are used simultaneously in conversations.

► **Note:** Includes staging suggestions, floor plans, and notes for teachers and directors.

► **Note:** Based on *Don Quixote* by Cervantes.

You're On! Seven Plays in English and Spanish

► **Author:** Plays selected by Lori Marie Carlson

► **Publication:** New York: Morrow Junior Books, 1999

► **LC#:** 99017222

► **Editions:**
0688162371 lib. bdg.

► **Description:** 139 pages, 24 cm. Cover illustration by Raul Colón.

► **Subjects:**

Children's plays, American—Hispanic-American authors
Children's plays, American—Hispanic-American authors—Translations into Spanish
Children's plays, Spanish
Children's plays, Spanish—Translations into English
Hispanic Americans—Juvenile drama
Plays—Collections
Plays—Hispanic American authors—Collections
Spanish-language materials—Bilingual

► **Interest Level:** ages 9–12

► **Reviewed:** *Booklist, Horn Book*

► **Note:** English and Spanish.

► **Note:** Includes biographical information on the playwrights.

► **Contents:**

These Shoes of Mine = Estos zapatos míos by Gary Soto. Translated into Spanish by Osvaldo Blanco.

   Characters: Manuel, Mother, Angel (school bully), Elena (Manuel's sister), relatives, Tío José, Ceci (girl Manuel likes), partygoers

Setting: living room and bedroom of Manuel's house and a street in the neighborhood

Tropical Memories = Remembranzas tropicales by Pura Belpré. Translated from Spanish by Lori Marie Carlson.

    Characters: Grandfather, Carmencita (granddaughter), chorus, coffee plants

    Setting: a tropical orchard in Puerto Rico

Jump In = Ven a saltar by Denise Ruíz. Translated into Spanish by Osvaldo Blanco.

    Characters: Girls and boys ages 9-12 Loida, Johanna, Yasmin, Maritza, Ceci, Eddie, Ralphy, Cheo, Carmen (age 18), Johanna's mom

    Setting: A street in the barrio, kitchen

The Girl Who Waters Basil and the Very Inquisitive Prince = La niña que riega la albahaca y el príncipe preguntón by Federico García Lorca. Translated by Lori Marie Carlson.

    Characters: African man, shoemaker, prince, prince's page, Irene (shoemaker's daughter), three wise men

    Setting: A nineteenth century Spanish palace

    Note: A reconstruction of a lost play

    Note: "An old Andalusian story in three acts."

Luck = La buena suerte by Elena Castedo

    Characters: Two groups, any number of actors

    Setting: Imaginary mountain and valley

    Note: "A comedic play for children in three acts."

A Dream in the Road = Un sueño en el camino by Alfonsina Storni. Translated by Lori Marie Carlson.

    Characters: Boy, Charlie Chaplin, Little Red Riding Hood, Tifón (fat husband), Sisebuta (nagging wife), Pinocchio, Cinderella, Giant, Dwarf

    Note: A mime play.

Christmas Fantasy = Fantasia de Navidad by Oscar Hijuelos. Translated into Spanish by Osvaldo Blanco.

    Characters: Santa Claus, Mrs. Claus, Peachpit, Persimmon, Birdbrain, other elves, Rico Pollo (reporter), Dancer (reindeer), Birdman, Snow Fairie, Angel of Light

    Setting: Santa's workshop

Chapter 6

Latino Poetry and Anthologies

Poetry takes many forms. Although the number of poetry books by Latino writers that are written specifically for children and young adults is somewhat limited, those works that do exist are of high quality. Most Latino poets whose works for children or young adults are now in print spent years as struggling poets and published books of poetry for a general audience long before they were able to publish poetry for children or teens.

Only during the past decade have **any** poetry books for children and young adults by Latino writers been published. One of the first Latino poets to publish poetry for children or teens was Gary Soto. His *Canto Familiar* (1995) and *Neighborhood Odes* (1992) were published years after the author's first poetry books gained recognition. Pat Mora's *My Own True Name: New and Selected Poems for Young Adults, 1984–1999* was published in 2000 by Arte Público Press. Poets Francisco X. Alarcón and Juan Felipe Herrera have combined poetry with illustrations to produce excellent picture books.

Several noteworthy anthologies of Latino poetry, prose, and art for young people remain in print and are included here. The youngest poet represented in this section is still a teen herself! These trends indicate a bright future for Latino poets who are speaking to children and young adults. A list of general-audience anthologies is included at the end of this chapter.

Barrio Streets, Carnival Dreams: Three Generations of Latino Artistry

▶ **Author:** Lori Marie Carlson, editor
▶ **Publication:** New York: Henry Holt and Company, 1996
St. Martin's Press
▶ **LC#:** 95041317
▶ **Editions:**
0805041206 hc.
0805045848 pb. St. Martin's Press
▶ **Description:** 142 pages, illustrated, 22 cm.
▶ **Summary:** A collection of Latino literature, poetry, artwork, and commentary celebrating the contributions of three generations of twentieth-century Americans of Mexican, Caribbean, and South American descent.
▶ **Subjects:**
American literature—Hispanic-American authors—Collections
Children's literature, American—Hispanic-American authors
Hispanic Americans—Juvenile literature
Hispanic Americans—Literary collections
Hispanic Americans in art
▶ **Series:** Edge books
▶ **Interest Level:** young adult
▶ **Note:** Includes works by Magdalena Hijuelos, Felipe Galindo-Feggo, Felipe Alfau, Marcos Rizo, José Martí, Pura Belpré, Louis Agassiz Fuertes, Susan Lowell, Oscar Hijuelos, Raúl Niño, David Hernandez, Albert Rivera, Jaime Manrique, Patricia Quintana, John Storm Roberts, Lyda Aponte de Zacklin, Rosie Perez, Raquel Jaramillo, Johanna Vega, Rebeca SanAndrés, Carlos Cumpián, Ricardo Estanislao Zulueta, Elias Zacklin, Jaime Hernandez, Regina Córdova, Demetria Martínez, Jeffry D. Scott.
▶ **Note:** Divided into three sections: América, Barrio Streets, and Carnival Dreams.

Canto Familiar

▶ **Author:** Gary Soto
▶ **Publication:** San Diego: Harcourt Brace & Co., 1995
▶ **LC#:** 94024218
▶ **Editions:**
0152000674 lib. bdg.
▶ **Description:** 79 pages, color illustrations, 24 cm. Illustrated by Annika Nelson.
▶ **Summary:** Twenty-five poems about the pleasures and woes that Mexican-American children experience growing up.
▶ **Subjects:**
American poetry
Children's poetry, American
Mexican-American children—Juvenile poetry
Mexican Americans—Poetry
▶ **Interest Level:** ages 9–12, grades 4–6
▶ **Reviewed:** *Booklist, Horn Book*
▶ **Note:** Full-page color illustrations

Cool Salsa: Bilingual Poems on Growing Up Latino in the United States

- ► **Editor:** Lori M. Carlson
- ► **Publication:** New York: H. Holt and Co., 1994
- ► **LC#:** 93045798
- ► **Editions:**
  08031359 hc.
  0449970436X pb. reprint, Juniper
- ► **Description:** 143 pages, 22 cm. Cover illustration by Emily Lisker. Pb: 158 pages.18 cm.
- ► **Subjects:**
  American poetry—Hispanic-American authors
  Children's poetry, American—Hispanic-American authors
  Children's poetry, Hispanic American (Spanish)—Translations into English
  Children's poetry, American—Hispanic-American authors—Translations into Spanish
  Hispanic-American children—Juvenile poetry
  Hispanic-American youth—Juvenile poetry
  Hispanic Americans—Juvenile poetry
- ► **Interest Level:** age 10 & up, grades 7–12, young adult
- ► **Reading Level:** 7
- ► **Reviewed:** *Booklist, Horn Book, Kirkus, Publishers Weekly, School Library Journal*
- ► **Lists:** ALA Best Books for Young Adults, ALA Outstanding Books for the College Bound, ALA Popular Paperbacks for Young Adults, *Horn Book* Fanfare, *Hungry Mind Review* Children's Books of Distinction, Notable Children's Trade Books in the Field of Social Studies (NCSS-CBC), *School Library Journal* Best Books

- ► **Note:** Introduction by Oscar Hijuelos
- ► **Note:** Poets are Mexican American, Cuban American, Puerto Rican, Argentine, Salvadoran, Bolivian American, Venezuelan, Colombian, Mexican, and Central American. Authors include: Luis Alberto Ambroggio, Ana Castillo, Sandra Castillo, Alfredo Chacón, Sandra Cisneros, Alberto Cano Correa, Ramón del Castillo, Abelardo Delgado, Alicia Gaspar de Alba, Martín Espada, Oscar Hijuelos, Carolina Hospital, Pablo Medina, Berta Montalvo, Pat Mora, Cristina Moreno, Amado Nervo, Judith Ortiz Cofer, Pedro Pietri, Claudia Quiróz, Daniel Jácome Roca, Luis J. Rodríguez, Trinidad Sánchez, Jr., Gary Soto, Alfonso Quijada Urías, Gina Valdés, E. J. Vega, Johanna Vega, and Ricardo Means Ybarra.
- ► **Note:** Contents are divided into categories: School Days, Home and Homeland, Memories, Hard Times, Time to Party, and A Promising Future.
- ► **Note:** Some poems appear along with translations. A glossary is provided. Includes short biographical sketches.

Here Is My Kingdom:

Hispanic-American Literature and Art for Young People

▶ **Author:** Charles Sullivan, editor
▶ **Publication:** New York: H. N. Abrams, 1994
▶ **LC#:** 93037412
▶ **Editions:**
  0810934221 hc.
▶ **Description:** 119 pages, illustrated, 27 cm.
▶ **Subjects:**
  American literature—Hispanic-American authors—Collections
  Children's literature, American—Hispanic-American authors
  Hispanic Americans—Juvenile literature
  Hispanic Americans—Literary collections
  Hispanic Americans in art
  Hispanic Americans in art—Juvenile literature
▶ **Interest Level:** grades 7–12, young adult
▶ **Reviewed:** *Booklist*, *The Book Report*
▶ **Lists:** New York Public Library's Books for the Teen Age
▶ **Note:** Foreword by Luis R. Cancel, Commissioner of Cultural Affairs, New York City.
▶ **Note:** Includes art or writing by Rudolfo Anaya, Homero Aridjis, Miranda Bergman, Rosario Castellanos, César Chávez, Eduardo Chávez, Judith Ortiz Cofer, Christopher Columbus, Hernán Cortés, Jack Delano, Daniel DeSiga, Bernal Díaz del Castillo, Richard Duardo, Roberto Durán, El Greco, Martin Espada, Sandra María Esteves, Hjalmar Flax, John Florez, Harry Fonseca, Ernesto Galarza, Odilia Galván Rodríguez, Daniel Gálvez, Miguel A. Gandert, Antonio E. García, Mario T. García, Rupert García, Rita Geada, Guillermo Gómez-Peña, Rebecca Gonzales, Rodolfo "Corky" Gonzales, Barbara Renaud González, Ray González, Jorge Guitart, Vicente Huidobro, Luis Jiménez, Raquel Jodorowsky, Frida Kahlo, Wilfredo Lam, Julio Larraz, Pedro Lastra, Fernando Leal, Roberto Lima, Miguel Linares, Carmen Lomas Garza, Alonzo Lopez, Circe Maia, Emanuel Martinez, Roberto Matta, Octavio Medellin, Luis Medina, Nicholasa Mohr, Malaquias Montoya, Pat Mora, Gerardo Mosquera, Manuel Neri, Luis Felipe Noe, José Clemente Orozco, Octavio Paz, Gustavo Pérez-Firmat, Pablo Picasso, Piri Thomas, Leroy V. Quintana, Joe B. Ramos, Diego Rivera, Francis Rivera, Tomás Rivera, Gonzalo Rojas, Orlando Romero, María Sabina, Rubén Salazar, Hugo Salazar Tamariz, Sebastião Salgado, Luis Omar Salinas, Carmen Tafolla, Rufino Tamayo, Anita Gonzáles Thomas, Francisco Toledo, Salvador Roberto Torres, Joaquín Torres-García, Rafael Tufiño, Sabine R. Ulibarrí, Cintio Vitier, and others.
▶ **Note:** Includes index and biographical notes.

Hispanic, Female and Young:
An Anthology

▶ **Author:** Phyllis Tashlik, editor
▶ **Publication:** Houston, TX: Piñata Books, 1994
▶ **LC#:** 93004101
▶ **Editions:**
1558850724 pb.
1558850805 pb.
0613028945 lib. bdg. Econo-Clad
▶ **Description:** 221 pages. 23 cm. Cover illustration by Gladys Ramírez.
▶ **Contents:** Nine chapters:
Remembering Our Culture
Lo Mágico y La Realidad
La Familia
Recuerdo: Memories from Childhood
Growing Up
A Las Mujeres
El Barrio
Prejudice
Making It (interviews with Ingrid Ramos, Olga Méndez, Nicholasa Mohr, and Tina Ramírez)
▶ **Subjects:**
American literature—20th century
American literature—Hispanic-American authors
Hispanic-American women—Literary collections
Hispanic-American youth—Literary collections
▶ **Interest Level:** grades 6–10, young adult
▶ **Reviewed:** *Booklist*
▶ **Lists:** ALA Quick Picks for Reluctant Young Adult Readers, New York Public Library's Books for the Teen Age, 1995

▶ **Note:** Contains poems, stories, essays by eighth-grade girls in a New York City public school who responded to the writings of Nicholasa Mohr, Pat Mora, Judith Ortiz Cofer, and others.
▶ **Note:** Includes a bibliography.

Laughing Out Loud, I Fly:
Poems in English and Spanish

▶ **Author:** Juan Felipe Herrera
▶ **Publication:** New York: HarperCollins Publishers, 1998
▶ **LC#:** 96045476
▶ **Editions:**
0060276045 hc.
0060276053 lib. bdg.
▶ **Description:** 48 pages, 19 cm. Cover illustration and interior drawings by Karen Barbour.
▶ **Summary:** A collection of poems in Spanish and English about childhood, place, and identity.
▶ **Subjects:**
American poetry
Children's poetry, American—Translations into Spanish
Herrera, Juan Felipe—Translations into Spanish
Mexican Americans—Juvenile poetry
Mexican Americans—Poetry
Spanish-language materials—Bilingual
▶ **Interest Level:** grades 5–9, young adult
▶ **Reading Level:** 6
▶ **Reviewed:** *Kirkus, School Library Journal*

- ▶ **Awards:** Pura Belpré honor book for narrative 2000
- ▶ **Note:** Spanish and English poems on facing pages.
- ▶ **Note:** An author's note at the end of the book explains his inspiration for writing this book of poems.

Mi'ja, never lend your mop...and other poems

- ▶ **Author:** Brigid Aileen Milligan
- ▶ **Publication:** San Antonio, TX: M&A Editions, 1999
- ▶ **LC#:** not available
- ▶ **Editions:**
  0930324641 pb.
- ▶ **Description:** 44 pages. 22 cm.
- ▶ **Summary:** The first collection of poetry by a recipient of the Hispanic Heritage Awards Foundation's 1999–2000 literature/journalism prize.
- ▶ **Contents:**
  Mi'ja, Never Lend Your Mop…
  Old Coffee Table: A Cracked Villanelle
  Silver Thread
  Destiny, please come to the front desk
  Insult
  Soy la pequeña
  Metal Plate
  Her Phaethon
  Cogitator's Work
  Discussions with a Deity
  Tendencies
  "I…,"
  Only Light
  More than Any Other
  6 a.m. Tortilla Lessons
  Forty Days
  Adobe Mamá
  Nuclear Physics Barbie
  Quirks
- ▶ **Subjects:**
  American poetry
  American poetry—Hispanic American authors
  Hispanic Americans—Poetry
  Mexican Americans—Poetry
- ▶ **Interest Level:** young adult
- ▶ **Reviewed:** *Dallas Morning News, REFORMA Newsletter*
- ▶ **Awards:** Tomás Rivera award nominee 2000
- ▶ **Note:** Written when the author was a senior in high school
- ▶ **Note:** M&A Editions distributed by Wings Press, 627 E. Guenther, San Antonio, TX 78210, Web site: <www.wingspress.com>
- ▶ **Note:** Back cover features statements from Marjorie Agosín, Carmen Tafolla, and Angela de Hoyos.

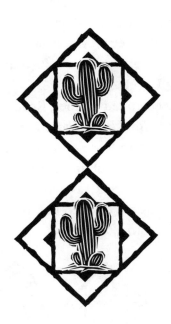

My Own True Name: New and Selected Poems for Young Adults, 1984–1999

- ▶ **Author:** Pat Mora
- ▶ **Publication:** Houston, TX: Piñata Books, 2000
- ▶ **LC#:** 00023969
- ▶ **Editions:**
  1558852921 pb.
- ▶ **Description:** 81 pages, illustrated, 22 cm. Illustrated by Anthony Accardo.
- ▶ **Summary:** More than 60 poems, some with Spanish translations, include such titles as "The Young Sor Juana," "Graduation Morning," "Border Town 1938," "Legal Alien," "Abuelita Magic," and "In the Blood."
- ▶ **Subjects:**
  American poetry
  Mexican Americans—Juvenile poetry
  Mexican Americans—Poetry
  Young adult poetry, American
- ▶ **Interest Level:** grades 7–12, young adult
- ▶ **Reading Level:** 5.9, 7.1
- ▶ **Tests:** Accelerated Reader, Reading Counts
- ▶ **Reviewed:** *Booklist, School Library Journal*
- ▶ **Awards:** Tomás Rivera nominee 2000
- ▶ **Lists:** New York Public Library's Books for the Teen Age, Texas Tayshas 2001–2002.
- ▶ **Note:** Poems are divided into three sections: Blooms, Thorns, and Roots.

Neighborhood Odes

- ▶ **Author:** Gary Soto
- ▶ **Publication:** San Diego: Harcourt Brace Jovanovich, 1992, 1994
- ▶ **LC#:** 91020710
- ▶ **Editions:**
  0152568794 lib. bdg.
  0590473352 pb. Point
  0785724966 lib. bdg. Econo-Clad
- ▶ **Description:** 68 pages, 24 cm. Illustrated by David Diaz.
- ▶ **Summary:** Twenty-one poems about growing up in an Hispanic neighborhood, highlighting the delights in such everyday items as sprinklers, the park, the library, and pomegranates.
- ▶ **Subjects:**
  American poetry
  Children's poetry, American
  Hispanic Americans—Juvenile poetry
  Hispanic Americans—Poetry
  Neighborhood—Juvenile poetry
  Neighborhood—Poetry
- ▶ **Interest Level:** ages 9–12, 10–12
- ▶ **Reading Level:** 5.3
- ▶ **Tests:** Reading Counts
- ▶ **Reviewed:** *Horn Book, Kirkus, Publishers Weekly, School Library Journal, VOYA*
- ▶ **Lists:** ALA Popular Paperbacks for Young Adults
- ▶ **Note:** Contains a glossary.

Vatos: Hymn to Vatos Who Will Never Be in a Poem

▶ **Author:** Luis Alberto Urrea
▶ **Photographer:** José Gálvez
▶ **Publication:** El Paso, TX: Cinco Puntos Press, 2000
▶ **LC#:** 00022409
▶ **Editions:**
0938317520 pb.
▶ **Description:** 95 pages. Illustrated with black-and-white photographs. 21 x 26 cm.
▶ **Subjects:**
Hispanic Americans—Portraits
Photography of men
Portrait photography
▶ **Interest Level:** young adult
▶ **Lists:** ALA Quick Picks for Reluctant Young Adult Readers nominee 2002
▶ **Note:** Foreword by Benjamin Alire Sáenz
▶ **Note:** Cover quotation by Edward James Olmos calls this a tribute to Chicano men, Latino men, and men everywhere.

Wáchale! Poetry and Prose on Growing Up Latino in America

▶ **Editor:** Ilan Stavans
▶ **Publication:** Chicago: Cricket Books, 2001
▶ **LC#:** 2001047189
▶ **Editions:**
0812647505 hc.

▶ **Description:** 160 pages, illustrated, 22 cm.
▶ **Summary:** A bilingual collection of poems, stories, and other writings that celebrate diversity among Latinos.
▶ **Contents:**
Part I. Rápido, Rápido
Part II. Rootas
Part III. P'atrás y P'alante
Part IV. Speakin' La Voz
▶ **Subjects:**
American literature—Hispanic-American authors—Collections
Children's literature, American—Hispanic-American authors
Children's literature, Latin American
Hispanic Americans—Juvenile literature
Hispanic Americans—Literary collections
Spanish-language materials—Bilingual
▶ **Interest Level:** ages 10–13, young adult
▶ **Note:** Includes a bibliography and a glossary.
▶ **Note:** Includes works by Rosaura Sánchez, Judith Ortiz Cofer, Carolina Hospital, Cecilio García-Camarillo, Gary Soto, Alcina Lubitch Domecq, José Martí, Martin Hoffman, Woody Guthrie, Luis Palés Matos, Jovita González, Jesús Colón, Manuel Gamio, Ricardo Pau-Llosa, Virgil Suárez, Martín Espada, Ruth Behar, Pat Mora, Dionisio D. Martínez, Ilan Stavans, Rolando Hinojosa-Smith, Willie Perdomo, Michele Serros, Luis J. Rodríguez, Achy Obejas, Alberto Alvaro Ríos, María Eugenia Morales, Nash Candelaria, Aurora Levins Morales, and Demetria Martínez.

¡Word Up! Hope for Youth Poetry from El Centro De La Raza

- ▶ **Editor:** Zoë Anglesey
- ▶ **Publication:** Seattle, WA: El Centro de la Raza, 1992.
- ▶ **LC#:** 92090571
- ▶ **Editions:**
  0963327518 pb.
- ▶ **Description:** 123 pages. 21 cm.
- ▶ **Subjects:**
  American poetry—20th Century
  American poetry—Hispanic-American authors
  American poetry—Washington (State)—Seattle
  Children's writings, American—Washington (State)—Seattle
  Hispanic-American children—Poetry
  School verse, American—Washington (State)—Seattle
- ▶ **Interest Level:** middle school, young adult
- ▶ **Note:** Poems produced in a poetry workshop conducted at El Centro de la Raza, a Chicano-Latino civil rights organization in Seattle, Washington.
- ▶ **Note:** Includes poems by 40 young poets. Most poems are one page or less in length. Some poems are in Spanish, some in English, and some in both languages.

Other Latino-authored Anthologies

This bibliography contains titles of anthologies written for a general audience or for adult readers. Some may contain materials that are not suitable for younger or less mature readers.

Boricuas: Influential Puerto Rican Writings—An Anthology. Edited by Roberto Santiago. Ballantine Books, 1995. 355 pages.

Las Christmas: escritores latinos recuerdan las tradiciones navideñas. Edited by Esmeralda Santiago and Joie Davidow. Vintage, 1998. 240 pages.

Las Christmas: Favorite Latino Authors Share Their Holiday Memories. Edited by Esmeralda Santiago and Joie Davidow. Knopf, 1998. 198 pages.

Growing Up Chicana/o: An Anthology. Edited by Tiffany Ana López. Morrow, 1993. 272 pages.

Hispanic American Literature: A Brief Introduction and Anthology. Edited by Nicolás Kanellos. Addison-Wesley, 1995. 351 pages.

Iguana Dreams: New Latino Fiction. Edited by Delia Poey and Virgil Suárez. HarperPerennial, 1992. 400 pages.

In Other Words: Literature by Latinas of the United States. Edited by Roberta Fernández. Arte Público Press, 1994. 554 pages.

Infinite Divisions: An Anthology of Chicana Literature. Edited by Tey Diana Rebolledo and Eliana S. Rivero. University of Arizona Press, 1993. 393 pages.

Latina: Women's Voices from the Borderlands. Edited by Lillian Castillo-Speed. Touchstone Books, 1995. 284 pages.

The Latino Reader: An American Literary Tradition from 1542 to the Present. Edited by Harold Augerbraum and Margarita Fernandez Olmos. Houghton Mifflin, 1997. 522 pages.

Little Havana Blues: A Cuban-American Literature Anthology. Edited by Delia Poey and Virgil Suárez. Arte Público Press, 448 pages.

Las Mamis: Favorite Latino Authors Remember Their Mothers. Edited by Esmeralda Santiago and Joie Davidow. Knopf, 2000. 191 pages.

Las Mamis: Escritores latinos recuerdan a sus madres. Translated by Nina Torres-Vidal. Vintage, 2001. 198 pages.

Mexican American Literature. Edited by Charles Tatum. Harcourt Brace, 1990. 710 pages.

Mirrors Beneath the Earth: Short Fiction by Chicano Writers. Edited by Ray González. Curbstone Press, 1992. 331 pages.

Noche Buena: Hispanic American Christmas Stories. Edited by Nicolas Kanellos. Oxford University Press, 2000. 370 pages.

Pieces of the Heart: New Chicano Fiction. Edited by Gary Soto. Chronicle Books, 1993. 192 pages.

The Prentice-Hall Anthology of Latino Literature. Edited by Eduardo E. del Rio. Prentice Hall, 2001. 544 pages.

Puerto Rican Writers at Home in the USA: An Anthology. Edited by Faythe Turner. Open Hand, 1991. 352 pages.

Short Fiction by Hispanic Writers of the United States. Edited by Nicolas Kanellos Arte Público Press, 1993. 285 pages.

Short Stories by Latin American Women: The Magic and the Real. Edited by Celia C. de Zapata. Arte Público Press, 1990. 224 pages.

Latino Nonfiction

Because some outstanding biographies and other nonfiction works by Latinos have appeared in recent years, some nonfiction books are included in this guide. Because of the number of subject areas involved, an alternative format has been used for Chapter 7. **Books that are specifically for children or young adults are indicated by an asterisk (*) before the title.**

Books in the nonfiction section are arranged in a modified Dewey Decimal System order using a brief format that includes title, author, series, Library of Congress numbers, International Standard Book Numbers, number of pages, illustrations, and book size. Glossaries, bibliographies, and indexes are indicated. Available interest and reading levels are listed. If a book has received or been nominated for a major award, that information also is indicated. Relevant reviews are listed; however, excellent books are occasionally overlooked, so a lack of reviews should not necessarily be considered as negative.

Subject headings have been modified and condensed in the interest of conserving space. Since the subject of this guide is "Latinos" or "Hispanic Americans," these subjects have been omitted to avoid redundancy. Relevant ethnic subject headings such as "Puerto Ricans" have been retained.

Some of the books in this section are written for adult or general audiences and may not be appropriate for younger readers. However, in the interest of providing a wider range of materials for young adults and more mature readers, these titles have been included. Additional lists of Latino authors of novels, short stories, drama, and poetry are included in Chapter 10. Because of the broad coverage of "nonfiction," non-listing of a title should not be considered a negative factor.

001-099 General Works

▶ **051-059 Serial Publications**
The Success of Hispanic Magazine: A Publishing Success Story, by John García. Photographs by Ricardo Vargas. 95038612. 0802783090 hc. 0802783104 lib. bdg. Walker, 1996. 84 pages, illustrated, 25 cm. glossary, bibliography, index. IL: grades 9–12. *Hispanic Magazine*. Periodicals, publishing.

▶ **070-079 Journalism**
American Chica: Two Worlds, One Childhood, by Marie Arana. 00047529. 0385319622 hc. Dial Press, 2001. 320 pages, 22 cm. National Book Award nominee 2001, *Library Journal* Best Books of 2001. *Booklist*, *Library Journal*, *Publishers Weekly*. Journalists, mixed heritage, Peru.

100-199 Philosophy

▶ **170-179 Ethics**
It's All in the Frijoles: 100 Famous Latinos Share Real-Life Stories, Time-Tested Dichos, Favorite Folktales, and Inspiring Words of Wisdom, edited by Yolanda Nava. 00024858. 0684849003 pb. Fireside, 2000. 331 pages. 22 cm. bibliography, index. Topics: responsibility, respect, loyalty, faith, honesty, courage, humility, and others.

200-299 Religions

Madonas de/of Mexico, by Diane de Avalle-Arce and Alma Muñoz Maya. Illustrated by Nancy Conkle. 0883882221 pb. Bellerophon Books, 2000. 48 pages, black-and-white full-page drawings, 28 cm. Bilingual text. Catholic Church, Christian saints, Mexico—history, saints, southwest U.S.—history.

300-399 Social Sciences

▶ ## 300-319 Social Sciences

Americanos: Latino Life in the United States: La Vida Latina en los Estados Unidos, by Edward James Olmos, Lea Ybarra, Manuel Monterrey. 98051930. 0316649147 hc. Little, 1999. 0316649090 pb. 176 pages, black-and-white and color photographs, 31 cm. *Booklist.* Hispanic Americans.

*Barrio Boy, by Ernesto Galarza. University of Notre Dame, 1971. 70146805. 0268004412 pb. 0833508210 lib. bdg. Econo-Clad. 282 pages. 321 pages. RL: 6.8, IL: 9—adult. Accelerated Reader, Reading Counts. Mexican Americans.

*Crews: Gang Members Talk to María Hinojosa, with photographs by German Perez. 94012173. 015292873 hc. 0152002839 pb. Harcourt, 1995. 168 pages, photographs, 22 cm. IL: young adult. ALA Popular Paperbacks for Young Adults nominee 2002.

De Colores Means All of Us: Latina Views for a Multi-Colored Century, by Elizabeth Martínez. 98006841. 089608583X pb. 0896085848 hc. South End, 1998. 266 pages, 22 cm. index. Culture.

Drink Cultura: Chicanismo, by José Antonio Burciaga. 92032614. 1877741078 pb. Joshua Odell, 1993. 145 pages *Library Journal.* Mexican Americans, Southwest.

*The Great Migration: From Farms to Cities, by Richard Sanchez. *Hispanic Heritage* series, vol. 5. 94023398. 1562393359 lib. bdg. 1562393855 pb. Abdo, 1994. 32 pages, color illustrations, 26 cm. bibliography, glossary. index. IL: ages 9–12, grades 4–6, RL: 5.9. Accelerated Reader. *School Library Journal.* Cuba, migrations, World War I, World War II, Mexican Revolution.

How Did You Get to Be Mexican? A White/Brown Man's Search for Identity, by Kevin Johnson. 98011811. 1566396506 hc. 1566396514 pb. Temple, 1998. 256 pages, bibliography, index. *Kirkus.* Mexican Americans, racially mixed people, race relations.

*Latinas: Hispanic Women in the United States, by Hedda Garza. Foreword by James D. Cockcroft. 2001027812. 082632360X pb. University of New Mexico, 2001. 192 pages. 24 cm. source notes, bibliography, index. ALA Best Books for Young Adults.

Latinos in Museums: A Heritage Reclaimed, edited by Antonio Ríos-Bustamante and Christine Marin. *Public History* series. Krieger, 1998. 159 pages, black-and-white photographs, 24 cm. bibliography, index. Other authors: Martha Gutierrez-Steinkamp, Karen Mary Davalos, E. Liane Hernandez, Cynthia E. Orozco, Theresa Chávez, and Reina Alejandra Prado Saldivar. Museums.

*Una Linda Raza: Cultural and Artistic Traditions of the Hispanic Southwest, by Angel Vigil. Foreword by Rudolfo Anaya. 97024290. 1555919588 pb. Fulcrum, 1998. 256 pages, black-and-white drawings, 28 cm. bibliography. index. IL: grades 4–8.

Spilling the Beans, by José Antonio Burciaga. 95068912. 1877741116 pb. Joshua Odell, 1995. 215 pages, illustrated, 19 cm. California, Mexican-American border region.

The Way It Was and Other Writings, by Jesús Colón. Edited by Edna Acosta-Belén and Virginia Sánchez Korrol. 92042443. 1558850570 pb. Arte Público, 1993. 127 pages, illustrated, bibliography. New York, Puerto Ricans.

► ## 320-329 Political Sciences

*The Fight for Civil Rights and a New Freedom, by Richard Sanchez. *Hispanic Heritage* series, vol. 6. 94023397. 1562393367 hc. 1562393863 pb. Abdo, 1994. 32 pages, color illustrations, 26 cm. glossary, bibliography, index. IL: ages 9–12, grades 4–6, RL: 6.0. Accelerated Reader. *School Library Journal.*

Memories of Chicano History: The Life and Narrative of Bert Corona, by Mario T. García. *Latinos in American Society and Culture* series. 92041578. 0520201523 pb. University of California, 1994. 378 pages, illustrated, bibliography, index. *Booklist, Chicago Tribune, Santa Barbara News Press.* Labor leaders, Mexican Americans.

► ## 330-339 Economics

*Best Careers for Bilingual Latinos: Market Your Fluency in Spanish to Get Ahead on the Job, by Graciela Kenig. 98030744. 0844245410. VGM, 1999. 238 pages. 23 cm. IL: young adult. *School Library Journal.*

*Jessie De La Cruz: Profile of a United Farm Worker, by Gary Soto. 00038520. 0892552530 hc. Persea, 2000. 116 pages, photographs, 22 cm. bibliography, index. IL: grade 6 & up, 7–12, young adult. *Booklist, School Library Journal.* Agricultural laborers, labor leaders, Mexican Americans, women.

▶ 360-369 Social Problems

Always Running: La Vida Loca: Gang Days in L. A., by Luis J. Rodríguez. 93044386. 0671882317 pb. 0613013239 lib. bdg. Econo-Clad. Curbstone, 1993. 92039002. Simon, 1994. 18926003012 abridged audiocassette Audiolibros del Mundo. 260 pages. RL: 7, IL: 7–12. ALA Outstanding Books for the College Bound, ALA Popular Paperbacks for Young Adults nominee 2002. *VOYA*. California, gangs, Los Angeles, Mexican Americans, youth. <www.barriolife.com/stories/running8.html>

East Side Dreams, by Art Rodríguez. 97078013. 1891823019 pb. 99093257. 0967155509 pb. Chusma, 1997. Dream House, 1999. 267 pages, illustrated, 22 cm. *Low Rider Magazine*. California, gang members, youth.

Two Badges: The Lives of Mona Ruiz, by Mona Ruiz and Geoff Boucher. 97022173. 1558852026 hc. Arte, 1997. 288 pages, 23 cm. California, gangs, law enforcement, policewomen, youth.

Lost in the System: Miss Teen USA's Triumphant Fight to Claim a Family of Her Own, by Charlotte Lopez with Susan Dworkin. 96002374. 0684811995 pb. Fireside/Simon & Schuster, 1996. 189 pages, illustrated with black-and-white photographs, 22 cm. Beauty contestants, foster children, Vermont.

▶ 370-379 Education

A Darker Shade of Crimson: Odyssey of a Harvard Chicano, by Ruben Navarrette, Jr. 93007985. 0553089986 hc. 0553374273 pb. reprint ed. 1994. Bantam, 1993. 287 pages, 24 cm. *Kirkus*. Education, higher education, Harvard University, Mexican Americans.

▶ 390-399 Customs

Digging the Days of the Dead: A Reading of Mexico's Días de muertos, by Juanita Garciagodoy. 98028489. 0870814990 hc. 0870815903 pb. University Press of Colorado, 1998. 333 pages, black-and-white and color illustrations, 23 cm. bibliography, index. *Library Journal*. Holidays, Mexico.

The Latino Holiday Book: From Cinco de Mayo to Día de los Muertos—The Celebrations and Traditions of Hispanic Americans, by Valerie Menard. Foreword by Cheech Marin. 00021889. 1569246467 pb. Marlowe, 2000. 190 pages, illustrated, 21 cm. bibliography. *Booklist*. Festivals.

Songs My Mother Sang to Me: An Oral History of Mexican American Women, by Patricia Preciado Martin. 92006745. 0816512795 hc. 0816513295 pb. University of Arizona, 1992. 225 pages, black-and-white photographs, 22 cm., index. Arizona, Mexican Americans, Sonora, Mexico, women.

"With His Pistol in His Hand," A Border Ballad and Its Hero, by Américo Paredes.
58010853. 0292701284 pb. University of Texas, 1958. 262 pages, illustrated, 23 cm. bibliography, index. *El corrido de Gregorio Cortez*. Gregorio Cortez.

400-499 Language

▶ ## 420-429 English, Anglo-Saxon Languages
Hunger of Memory: The Education of Richard Rodríguez, by Richard Rodríguez.
81081810. 0553272934 pb. 0785776982 lib. bdg. Econo-Clad. Godine, 1982.
195 pages RL: 7, 8.1, IL: 7-adult. Reading Counts. ALA Outstanding Books for the College
Bound. *Boston Globe, New York Times, Publishers Weekly, School Library Journal*.
Affirmative action, bilingual education, California, Mexican Americans.

500-599 Science

▶ ## 510-519 Mathematics
Jaime Escalante: Inspiring Educator, by Maritza Romero. 97011603. 0823950859 lib. bdg.
PowerKids, 1997. 24 pages, color illustrations, 19 x 20 cm., index. RL: 4.1, IL: K–3, gr.
2–3. Education, mathematics, teachers.

▶ ## 590-599 Zoology
*Coquí y sus Amigos: Los animales de Puerto Rico = Coquí and His Friends: The
Animals of Puerto Rico*, by Alfonso Silva Lee. 9931351. 192916503X pb. Pangaea, 2000.
Text in Spanish and English. 96 pages, color illustrations. IL: ages 9–12. Animals, bilingual,
Puerto Rico, zoology, Spanish-language materials.

Natural Puerto Rico = Puerto Rico natural, by Alfonso Silva Lee. 98009282. 096301806X
pb. Pangaea, 1998. 126 pages, color illustrations, 25 cm., index. Parallel text in English and
Spanish. Animals, bilingual, birds, insects, Puerto Rico, zoology.

600-609 Technology

Careers in Technology, by Kimberly García. *Latinos at Work* series: *Career Role Models for Young Adults*. 2001029887. 1584150874. Mitchell, 2001. 96 pages, black-and-white photographs, 25 cm. bibliography, index. Careers, technology.

620-629 Engineering

***Ellen Ochoa: The First Hispanic Woman Astronaut**, by Maritza Romero. 97011546. 0823950875 lib. bdg. PowerKids, 1997. 24 pages, illustrated, 19 cm., index. IL: grades 2–3, RL: 3.7–4.8. Accelerated Reader, Reading Counts. Astronauts, Mexican Americans, women.

640-649 Home Economics

***Cooking the Mexican Way**, by Rosa Coronado. 00011175. Revised edition. 0822541173 lib. bdg. 0822541629 pb. Lerner, 2001. 72 pages, illustrated, 23 cm. IL: ages 9–12, grades 5–12. Cookery, food.

Flora's Kitchen: Recipes from a New Mexico Family = La Cocina de Flora: Recetas de una Familia de Nuevo Mexico, by Regina Romero. 1887896104 pb. Treasure, 1998. 127 pages, illustrated, 22 cm. glossary. *New Mexico Magazine*. Cookery, food, Mexican Americans, New Mexico.

Puerto Rican Cookery: A New Approach of a Revised and Enlarged Edition of 'The Art of Caribbean Cookery,' by Carmen Aboy Valldejuli. 83002149. 0882894110. Pelican, 2000. 389 pages, illustrated, 23 cm., glossary, indexes (Spanish and English). *New York Times*. Cookery, food, Puerto Ricans.

Puerto Rican Cuisine in America: Nuyorican and Bodega Recipes, by Oswald Rivera. Illustrations by Carlos Frias. 92041478. 0941423840 pb. Four, 1993. 293 pages, 23 cm., glossary, index. Cookery, food, Puerto Ricans.

Recipe of Memory: Five Generations of Mexican Cuisine, by Victor M. Valle and Mary Lau Valle. 95010825. 1565841263. New Press, 1995. 186 pages, illustrated, 20 cm., index. *Houston Chronicle, Midwest Book Review, New York Daily News, L. A. Weekly*. Cookery, Guadalajara, Mexico, Mexican Americans.

Southwest Flavor: Adela Amador's Tales from the Kitchen, by Adela Amador. 00130648. 093720661X spiral binding. *New Mexico Magazine*, 2000. 150 pages, 20 x 17 cm. Cookery, food, Mexican Americans, New Mexico.

A Taste of Puerto Rico: Traditional and New Dishes from the Puerto Rican Community, by Yvonne Ortiz. 93046165. 0525938125 hc. 0452275482 pb. Plume, 1994, 1997. 284 pages, illustrated, 23 cm., index. *Booklist, Miami Herald, New York Times Book Review*. Cookery, food, Puerto Ricans.

700-799 Fine Arts and Recreation

▶ ### 730-739 Plastic Arts, Sculpture

Howl: The Artwork of Luis Jiménez, by Camille Flores-Turney. 98116990. 0937206482 hc. New Mexico, 1997. 75 pages, color & black-and-white illustrations, 23 x 28 cm. Art, Luis Jiménez, sculpture.

*Making Magic Windows: Creating Papel Picado/Cut-Paper Art with Carmen Lomas Garza. 9838518. 0892391596 pb. Children's, 1999. 61 pages, illustrated, 28 cm. "Provides instructions for making paper banners and more intricate cutouts. Includes diagrams." Handicraft, paper work.

▶ ### 740-749 Drawing and Decorative Arts

*The Piñata Maker = El Piñatero, by George Ancona. 93002389. 0152618759 hc. 0152000607 pb. Harcourt, 1994. 40 pages, color illustrations, 27 cm. IL: ages 7–9. *Booklist, Horn Book, Kirkus*. Bilingual, Mexico, paper work, piñatas, Spanish-language materials.

The Lower You Ride, the Cooler You Are: A Baldo Collection, by Hector Cantu and Carlos Castellanos. 2001087913. 0740718401 pb. Andrews McMeel Publishing, 2001. 128 pages, illustrated with drawings, 23 cm. Cartoons, comics.

▶ ### 750-759 Painting and Paintings

*Frida Kahlo, by Hedda Garza. *Hispanics of Achievement* series. 93002334. 0791016986 hc. 0791016994 pb. 0785771220 lib. bdg. Econo-Clad. Chelsea House, 1994. 120 pages, black-and-white illustrations, 25 cm., chronology, bibliography, index. IL: ages 9–12. Artists, painters, Mexico, *Horn Book*.

A Piece of My Heart = Pedacito de mi Corazon: The Art of Carmen Lomas Garza, by Carmen Lomas Garza. 156841646 pb. New, 1994. 62 pages, illustrated. Art, artists, Mexican Americans, Texas.

Soraida's Verdadism: The Intellectual Voice of a Puerto Rican Woman on Canvas: Unique, Controversial Images and Style, by Soraida Martinez. 99068364. 0967671906 pb. S. Martinez, 1999. 105 pages, color illustrations, 23 x 31 cm. Prejudice, identity, women, diversity, sexism, racism.

▶ 780-789 Music

Better Part of Me, by Jon Secada. Warner Bros. Publications, 2000. 076929538X pb. 87 pages, black-and-white photographs, printed music, 31 cm. Contains song lyrics and music to 14 songs by Secada. Music.
Note: Similar books of lyrics and music of other Latino musicians are available.

The Billboard Guide to Tejano and Regional Mexican Music, by Ramiro Burr. 98051910. 0823076911 pb. Billboard, 1999. 256 pages, black-and-white photographs, 24 cm., discography, index. Mexican Americans, music, popular music, Tejano music.

*Christina Aguilera: Young Singer, by Christine Granados. *Real-Life Reader Biography* series. 00044405. 1584150440 lib. bdg. Mitchell, 2001. 32 pages, illustrated, chronology, index. IL: grades 3–7, ages 9–12, RL: 6.1. Accelerated Reader. *Booklist.* Singers.

*Enrique Iglesias: Latino Pop Star, by Christine Granados. *A Real-Life Reader Biography* series. 00057711. 1587150459 lib. bdg. Mitchell, 2000. 32 pages, illustrated, 25 cm., discography, index. IL: ages 9--2, RL: 5.4. Accelerated Reader. *Booklist.* Singers.

*Gloria Estefan: Singer and Entertainer, by Doreen Gonzales. *Hispanic Biographies* series. 97042787. 0894908901 lib. bdg. Enslow, 1998. 182 pages, illustrated, 24 cm., discography, videography, bibliography, index. IL: grades 6–9, young adult, RL: 6.7. Accelerated Reader. *School Library Journal.* Cuban Americans, singers.

*Joan Baez, by Hedda Garza. *Hispanics of Achievement* series. 90044108. 0791012336 hc. 0791012603 pb. 0785771271 lib. bdg. Econo-Clad. Chelsea, 1991. 119 pages, illustrated, 25 cm., bibliography, index. IL: ages 9–12, RL: 8.2. Accelerated Reader.

*Joan Baez: Folksinger for Peace, by Maritza Romero. 97007432. 0823950840 lib. bdg. PowerKids, 1997. 24 pages, color illustrations, 19 x 20 cm., index. RL: 4.2, IL: K–3, grades 2–3. Accelerated Reader, Reading Counts. Political activists, singers.

Latin Sensations, by Herón Márquez. *Biography* series. 00008876. 082254993X lib. bdg. 0822596954 pb. Lerner 2001. 112 pages, illustrated, 23 cm., bibliography, discography, index. RL: 6, IL: ages 7–12, 9–12, grades 5–9. ALA Quick Picks for Reluctant Readers 2002 nominee. *School Library Journal.* Marc Anthony, Enrique Iglesias, Jennifer Lopez, Ricky Martin, Selena Perez, singers.

Marc Anthony, by John Torres. 00067665. 1584150696 hc. *Real-Life Reader Biography* series. Mitchell, 2002. 32 pages, illustrated, chronology, index. Singers.

Ricky Martin: Latin Entertainer, by Valerie Menard. *Real-Life Reader Biography* series. 9940617. 1584150599 lib. bdg. Mitchell, 2000. 32 pages, illustrated, discography, chronology, index. IL: ages 9–12, grades 1–5, RL: 6.2. Accelerated Reader. Puerto Ricans, singers.

Selena Perez: Queen of Tejano Music, by Maritza Romero. 97006730. 0823950867 lib. bdg. PowerKids, 1997. 24 pages, 19 x 20 cm., index. RL: 4.1, IL: K–3, grades 2–3. Accelerated Reader, Reading Counts. *School Library Journal.* Tejano musicians.

Sheila E.: Multi-Talented Female Percussionist, by Christine Granados. *Real-Life Reader Biographies* series. 9925254. 158415019X lib. bdg. Mitchell, 2000. 32 pages, illus. chronology, index. RL: 5.3, IL: grades 1–5. Accelerated Reader, Reading Counts. Musicians, percussionists, singers.

▶ ## 790-795 Performing Arts

Cheech Marin, by Valerie Menard. *Real-Life Reader Biography* series. 2001029088. 158415070X lib. bdg. Mitchell, 2002. 32 pages, illustrated, 24 cm., filmography, discography, index. Actors and actresses, Mexican Americans.

Cristina Saralegui: Journalist/Talk Show Host, by Valerie Menard. *Real-Life Reader Biography* series. 9743427. 1883845602 lib. bdg. Mitchell, 1998. 32 pages, illustrated, 24 cm., chronology, index. IL: grades 1–5, RL: 5.3. Accelerated Reader. Cuban Americans, television.

Hispanic Hollywood: The Latins in Motion Pictures, by George Hadley-García. 90048016. 0806511850 pb. (English) 0806512083 pb. (Spanish) Carol, 1990. 256 pages, illustrated, bibliography, index. Actors, motion pictures.

Hispanics in Hollywood: An Encyclopedia of 100 Years in Film and Television, by Luis Reyes and Peter Rubic. 00034884. 1580650252 pb. Lone, 2000. 607 pages, illustrated, bibliography. Actors, motion pictures, television.

Jennifer Lopez: Latina Singer/Actress, by Valerie Menard. *Real-Life Reader Biography* series. 00034923. 1584150254 lib. bdg. Mitchell, 2001. 32 pages, illustrated, filmography, discography, chronology, index. IL: grades 3–7, RL: 6.6. Accelerated Reader. *Booklist*. Actors, Puerto Ricans, singers.

Raul Julia: Actor and Humanitarian, by Bárbara Cruz. *Hispanic Biographies* series. 97037827. 0766010406 lib. bdg. Enslow, 1998. 182 pages, illustrated, 24 cm., chronology. IL: grade 9 & up, young adult, RL: 8. Accelerated Reader. *School Library Journal*. Actors, Puerto Ricans.

Rebel Without a Crew, or, How a 23-Year-Old Filmmaker with $7,000 Became a Hollywood Player, by Robert Rodríguez. 95023424. 0525937943 hc. 0452271878 pb. Plume, 1996. 301 pages, illustrated, 21 cm. Motion picture producers and directors, diary.

Salma Hayek, by Valerie Menard. *Real-Life Reader Biography* series. 99029471. 1584150181 lib. bdg. Mitchell, 2000. 32 pages, illustrated, 25 cm., filmography, index. Actors and actresses, Mexico.

► ## 796-799 Recreation Sports

Athletes Remembered: Mexicano/Latino Professional Football Players 1929-1970, by Mario Longoria. 96043251. 0927534630 pb. Bilingual, 1997. 196 pages, illustrated, bibliography, index. *Midwest Book Review*. Football players.

Bobby Bonilla by John A. Torres. *Latinos in Baseball* series. 98048050. 1883845831 lib. bdg. Mitchell, 1999. 64 pages, illustrated, 25 cm., index. IL: ages 9–12, RL: 6.2. Accelerated Reader. Baseball players.

Careers in Sports, by Valerie Menard. *Latinos at Work* series. 2001042775. 1584150866 lib. bdg. Mitchell, 2001. 96 pages, black-and-white photographs, 25 cm. Careers, sports.

Icebreaker: The Autobiography of Rudy Galindo, by Rudy Galindo and Eric Marcus. 97162449. 0671003909 hc. 0671003917 pb. 0613080424 lib. bdg. Econo-Clad. Pocket, 1997. 255 pages, illustrated. *Kirkus*. Gay men, Mexican Americans, skaters.

Oscar De La Hoya: Champion Boxer, by Valerie Menard. *Real-Life Reader Biography* series. 9743509. 1883845580 lib. bdg. Mitchell, 1998. 24 pages, illustrated, chronology, index. IL: grades 2–5, ages 9–12, RL: 5.4. Accelerated Reader, Reading Counts. Boxers, Mexican Americans.

The Quarterback Who Almost Wasn't, by Jorge Prieto. 93029314. 1558851097 pb. Arte, 1994. 128 pages, 22 cm. IL: grades 7–10, RL: 7.6. Accelerated Reader. *Booklist*. Football players, heart diseases, physicians.

Roberto Clemente: Baseball Hall of Famer, by Maritza Romero. 97004231. 0823950832 lib. bdg. PowerKids, 1997. 24 pages, illustrated, 19 cm., index. RL: 3.7, IL: K–3, grades 2–3. Accelerated Reader, Reading Counts. Baseball players, Pittsburgh Pirates, Puerto Ricans.

Tino Martinez, by John A. Torres. *Latinos in Baseball* series. 98048049 1883845823 lib. bdg. Mitchell, 1999. 64 pages, illustrated, 25 cm., index. IL: ages 9–12, RL: 6.3. Accelerated Reader. Baseball players.

Trent Dimas, by Valerie Menard and Sue Boulais. A *Real-Life Reader Biography*. 97021984. 1883845505 lib. bdg. Mitchell, 1998. 32 pages, illustrated, 24 or 25 cm. IL: grades 1–5, ages 9–12, RL: 5.5, 6.5. Accelerated Reader, Reading Counts. *Horn Book*. Gymnasts.

Viva Baseball! Latin Major Leaguers and Their Special Hunger, by Samuel O. Regalado. *Sport and Society* series. 97021066. 0252023722 hc. University of Illinois, 1998. 240 pages, illustrated, maps, bibliography, index. Baseball players.

800-899 Literature

► ## 810-818 American Literature

Buffalo Nickel: A Memoir, by Floyd Salas. 91048217. 155885049X hc. Arte, 1992. 250 pages. Boxers, brothers, families, novelists, suicide.

Capirotada: A Nogales Memoir, by Alberto Alvaro Ríos. 99030583. 0826320937 hc. 0826320945 pb. University of New Mexico, 1999. 148 pages, illustrated. *Booklist*. Authors, Mexican Americans, Nogales, Arizona.

House of Houses, by Pat Mora. Beacon Press, 1997. 96043948. 08070201X pb. 0613181182 lib. bdg. Econo-Clad. 324 pages, illustrated, 21 cm. ALA Outstanding Books for the College Bound. *Booklist, Kirkus, New York Times*. Families, Mexican Americans, poets.

I Can Hear the Cowbells Ring, by Lionel G. García. 94008658. 155885143 pb. Arte, 1994. 206 pages, 22 cm. Authors, families, Mexican Americans, Texas.

Living Up the Street: Narrative Recollections, by Gary Soto. 85009893. 0440211700 pb. Laurel. 0833581201 lib. bdg. Econo-Clad. Laurel, 1985. 159 pages, illustrated, 23 cm. IL: ages 9–12, young adult, RL: 7.5. Reading Counts. Mexican Americans, poets.

Man of Aztlan: A Biography of Rudolfo Anaya, by Abelardo Baeza. 2001040460. 1571685642. Eakin, 2001. 101 pages, illustrated, 23 cm., chronology, bibliography. Authors, Mexican Americans.

Memory Fever: A Journey Beyond El Paso del Norte, by Ray González. Camino del Sol series. 99030986. 0816520119 pb. University of Arizona, 1999. 240 pages. *Kirkus*. Authors, El Paso, Texas, Mexican Americans.

Nobody's Son: Notes from an American Life, by Luis Alberto Urrea. *Camino del Sol* series. 98008924. 0816518653 hc. University of Arizona, 1998. 190 pages. *Booklist*. Authors, Mexican Americans, Mexico, southwestern states.

Rain of Gold, by Victor Villaseñor. Arte Público Press, 1991. 1558850309 hc. 038531177X. pb. Delta, 1992. 562 pages. 0736634827 audiocassette, part 1, 0736634835, audiocassette, part 2. Books on Tape, 1996 *Kirkus, New York Times, Publishers Weekly*. Authors, California, families, Mexican Americans, Mexico.

*Silent Dancing: A Partial Remembrance of a Puerto Rican Childhood, by Judith Ortiz Cofer. 89077428. 1558850155 pb. 0613179781 lib. bdg. Econo-Clad. Arte, 1990. 168 pages, 21cm. *Bailando en silencio: Escenas de una niñez puertorriqueña*. Translated by Elena Olazagastie-Segovia. 97022156. 1558852050 pb. Piñata Books, 1997. 160 pages, 22 cm. Authors, Puerto Rico.

Spared Angola: Memories from a Cuban-American Childhood, by Virgil Suárez. 96039825. 1558851976 pb. Arte, 1997. 168 pages, 22 cm. Authors, Cuban Americans.

*A Summer Life, by Gary Soto. 89040614. 0440210240 pb. Laurel. 0833574736 lib. bdg. Econo-Clad. University Press of New England, 1990. 124 pages, 22 cm. RL: 7, IL: 7 & up. *Publisher's Weekly*. California, poets.

Thirteen Senses: A Memoir, by Victor Villaseñor. 2001275930. 0066210771 hc. Rayo, 2001. 523 pages, illustrated, 25 cm. HarperAudio 0694256614 abridged audiocassette, also available as a downloadable e-book. Spanish-language version *Trece Sentidos: Una Memoria* translated by Alfonso González. Sequel to *Rain of Gold. Publishers Weekly*. Authors, California, families, Mexican Americans.

*Under the Royal Palms: A Childhood in Cuba, by Alma Flor Ada. 97048887. 0689806310 lib. bdg. Atheneum, 1998. 88 pages, black-and-white photographs, 24 cm. IL: ages 9–12, 9–14, RL: 6.1, 6.6. Accelerated Reader, Reading Counts. *Horn Book, Kirkus, New York Times*. Authors, Cuba, Cuban Americans, families.

Urban Exile: Collected Writings of Harry Gamboa, Jr., edited by Chon A. Noriega. 98014991. 0816630518 hc. 0816630526 pb. University of Minnesota, 1998. 562 pages, black-and-white photographs, 26 cm. Art, California, Chicano Arts Movement, civil rights, Los Angeles, Mexican Americans.

*Walking Stars: Stories of Magic and Power, by Victor Villaseñor. 94007404. 1558851186 hc. 038531654 pb. Piñata Books, 1994. 202 pages. 0736633359 audiocassette. Delta. Books on Tape. IL: grades 7–12, young adult, RL: 5.6. Accelerated Reader. *Booklist, Horn Book*. Authors, Mexican Americans.

The Wild Steps of Heaven, by Victor Villaseñor. 0385315694 pb. Delta, 1997. 293 pages. 156100670X abridged cassette. 156100295X unabridged cassette. Brilliance, 1996. *Booklist*. Authors, Mexican Americans.

Working in the Dark: Reflections of a Poet of the Barrio, by Jimmy Santiago Baca. 91060328. 1878610082 hc. 1878610473 pb. Red Crane, 1992. 168 pages, *Multicultural Review*. Mexican Americans, poets, prison life, writing.

▶ **860-869 Spanish and Portuguese Literature**

*Sor Juana: A Trailblazing Thinker, by Elizabeth Coonrod Martinez. *Hispanic Heritage* series. 93015095. 1562944061 lib. bdg. Millbrook, 1994. 32 pages, back-and-white, color illustrations, 24 cm., bibliography, chronology, index. IL: ages 4–8. *Horn Book*. Authors, Juana Inés de la Cruz, sister, 1651–1695, Mexico, nuns.

900-999 Geography, Biography, History

▶ **910 Travel**

*Spain: Explorers & Conquerors, by Richard Sanchez. *Hispanic Heritage* series, vol. 2. 9417409. 1562393324 lib. bdg. Abdo, 1994. 32 pages, color illustrations, 26 cm., glossary, index. IL: ages 9–12, grades 4–6, RL: 5.6. Accelerated Reader. *School Library Journal*. Explorers, Fernando Cortez, Ponce De Leon, Francisco de Coronado, Portugal, Juan Rodríguez Cabrillo, Francisco Pizarro, Spain, Vasco Nunez de Balboa.

▶ **920 Collective biography**

Extraordinary People in Extraordinary Times: Heroes, Sheroes, and Villains, by Patrick M. Mendoza. 9914238. 1563086115 pb. Libraries, 1999. 142 pages, bibliography, index. Roy Benavidez, heroes, José Marti, women.

▶ **940-949 History of Europe**

Mayhem Was Our Business = Memorias de un veterano, by Sabine R. Ulibarrí. 96043060. 0927534649 pb. Bilingual, 1997. 115 pages. English and Spanish. Air pilots, military, United States, Army Air Forces, World War, 1939-1945.

▶ **950-959 History of Asia**

Aztlán and Viet Nam: Chicano and Chicana Experiences of the War, edited by George Mariscal. *American Crossroads* series. 98039737. 0520214048 hc. 0520214056 pb. University of California, 1999. 337 pages, 23 cm., bibliography. Mexican Americans, soldiers, Vietnamese Conflict.

Medal of Honor: One Man's Journey from Poverty and Prejudice, by Roy Perez Benavidez and John R. Craig. 94027283. 1574882031 pb. Batsford, 1999. 240 pages, 24 cm. Medal of Honor, soldiers, United States, Army, Vietnamese Conflict.

A Patriot After All: The Story of a Chicano Vietnam Vet, by Juan Ramirez. 98046679. 0826319599 pb. University of New Mexico, 1999. 192 pages. Latino Literary Hall of Fame, 2000. *Kirkus*. Mexican Americans, soldiers, Vietnamese Conflict.

Soldados: Chicanos in Viet Nam: Narratives of the Viet Nam War, edited by Charley Trujillo. 89081107. 0962453609 pb. Chusma, 1990. 187 pages, 22 cm. American Book Award 1991. Mexican Americans, personal narratives, soldiers.

▶ **970-979 History of North America**

*Ancient Empires & Mighty People, by Richard Sanchez. *Hispanic Heritage* series, vol. 1. 9415860. 1562393316 lib. bdg. Abdo, 1994. 32 pages, color illustrations, 26 cm., bibliography, glossary, index. IL: ages 9–12, grades 4–6, RL: 6.1. Accelerated Reader. *School Library Journal*. Antiquities, Aztecs, Incas, Indians, Mayans.

Barefoot Heart: Stories of a Migrant Child, by Elva Treviño Hart. 99011731. 0927534819 pb. Bilingual, 1999. 075315790X hc. (large print) 0753196247 pb. (large print) ISIS, 2000. 236 pages. RL: 5.7, IL: 7–adult. Accelerated Reader. *Library Journal, Publishers Weekly, School Library Journal*. Mexican Americans, migrant agricultural laborers, women.

Blessed by Thunder: Memoir of a Cuban Girlhood, by Flor Fernandez-Barrios. 99020902. 1580050425 pb. Seal, 1999. 252 pages, 23 cm. *Booklist, Los Angeles Times*. Cuba, Cuban Americans, refugees.

*Building a New World, by Richard Sanchez. *Hispanic Heritage* series, vol. 3. 94021879. 1562393332 lib. bdg. 1562393839 pb. Abdo, 1994. 32 pages, color illustrations, 26 cm.,

glossary, bibliography, index. IL: ages 9–12, grades 4–6, RL: 5.6. Accelerated Reader. *School Library Journal*. United States—Discovery and exploration, United States—History.

*Charro: The Mexican Cowboy, by George Ancona. 98013396. 0152010475 hc. 0152010467 pb. Harcourt, 1999. 48 pages, color illustrations, 27 cm. IL: ages 9–12, grades 4–6, RL:5.0 (Spanish) 5.3 (English). *Booklist, Horn Book*. Charros, cowboys, Mexico.

Chicano! The History of the Mexican American Civil Rights Movement, by Francisco A. Rosales. 96005979. 1558852018 pb. Arte, 1996. 326 pages, illustrated, 29 cm. Based on the four-part television series of the same name. *Book News, Booklist, Midwest Book Review*. Civil rights, Mexican Americans.

Everything You Need to Know about Latino History, by Himilce Novas. Revised edition. 98004354. 0452279917 pb. Plume, 1998. 368 pages, map, 21 cm., bibliography, index. *Booklist, Kirkus*. History.

*Hispanic American Almanac, edited by Bryan Ryan and Nicolás Kanellos. 95196496. 0810398230 hc. U X L, 1995. 234 pages, black-and-white photographs, 25 cm., bibliography, index. *Booklist, Book News, The Book Report*.

*Hispanic American Chronology, edited by Nicolás Kanellos and Bryan Ryan. 95042859. 0810398265 hc. U X L, 1996. 212 pages, black-and-white photographs, maps, 25 cm., bibliography, index. *The Book Report*. Portugal—History, Spain—History, United States—History.

The Hispanic Presence in North America from 1492 to Today, by Carlos M. Fernández-Shaw. Updated Edition. 98050718. 0816040109 hc. Facts, 1999. 415 pages, illustrated, maps, 29 cm., bibliography, index. *Book News, The Book Report, VOYA*. Spaniards—History, United States—Civilization.

*Kids Explore America's Hispanic Heritage, Westridge Young Writers Workshop. Second edition. 96002614. 0613081889 lib. bdg. 1562612727 pb. John Muir, 1996. 159 pages, illustrated, maps, 23 cm., index. IL: ages 9–12. "Writings by students in grades three to seven on dance, cooking, games, history, art, songs, and role models."

*The Mexican-American Experience, by Elizabeth Coonrod Martinez. *Coming to America* series. Millbrook, 1995. 64 pages, color and black-and-white illustrations, 27 cm., bibliography, index. IL: ages 9–12. *Horn Book*. Immigrants, Mexican Americans, United States—History.

The Monkey Box, by Art Rodríguez. 0967155517 pb. Dream, 1999. 148 pages, 22 cm. Families, Mexican Americans, Mexico—History.

The New York Public Library Amazing Hispanic American History, by George Ochoa. 98023797. 047119204X pb. John Wiley, 1998. 192 pages, illustrated, bibliography, index, maps, 23 cm. IL: ages 9–12. *Kirkus*. Cuban Americans, Mexican Americans, Puerto Ricans, United States—History.

Son of Two Bloods, by Vincent L. Mendoza. 95050326. 0803282575 pb. University of Nebraska, 1996. Bison Books, 1999. 200 pages, illustrated, 22 cm. North American Indian Prose Award. Creek Indians, Indians, mixed heritage.

The Story of Mexico: A Bellerophon Coloring Book = La Historia de México en Español y en Inglés: Un Libro Para Pintar, by Eric Tomb, Donna Neary, Elena López, Diane de Avalle-Arce. Illustrated by Nancy Conkle. Bellerophon Books, 2000. 0883881594 pb. 48 pages, black-and-white line drawings, 29 cm. Art, Aztecs, explorers, Mexico—History, Mexican Revolution, religion.

▶ ## 974.7 Puerto Ricans

Almost a Woman, by Esmeralda Santiago. 98086520. 0738200433. Perseus, 1998. 99025592. 037570521X pb. Vintage, 1999. 061324141X lib. bdg. Econo-Clad 320 pages, illustrated. RL: 6.9, IL: 7–adult. *Casi una mujer*, translated by Nina Torres-Vidal. 99033347. 0375705260 pb. Vintage, 1999. Accelerated Reader. ALA Popular Paperbacks for Young Adults nominee 2002. *Booklist*. New York, Puerto Ricans, women.

Down These Mean Streets, by Piri Thomas. 30th Anniversary edition. 98114757. 0679781420 pb. Vintage, 1997. 0808586734 lib. bdg. Econo-Clad. 350 pages. RL: 9, IL: 9–adult. Reading Counts. ALA Popular Paperbacks for Young Adults nominee 2002. Harlem, New York, Puerto Ricans.

Family Installments: Memories of Growing Up Hispanic, by Edward Rivera. 82002236. Morrow, 1982. 83003985. 0140067264 pb. Viking, 1983. 300 pages. New York, Puerto Ricans.

*Poet and Politician of Puerto Rico: Don Luis Muñoz Marin, by Carmen T. Bernier-Grand. 94021985. 0531068870 hc. 0531087379 lib. bdg. Orchard, 1995. 118 pages, black-and-white photographs, 24 cm., bibliography, index. IL: ages 9–12, grades 5–8. *Booklist, Horn Book*. Governors, Puerto Ricans, Puerto Rico—History, statesmen.

When I Was Puerto Rican, by Esmeralda Santiago. 94027087. 0679756760 pb. Vintage, 1994. 274 pages. *Cuando era puertorriqueña*. 94011467. 0679756779 pb. Vintage, 1994. 274 pages. ALA Popular Paperbacks for Young Adults nominee 2002. New York, Puerto Ricans, Puerto Rico.

▶ ## 976.4 Texas

Crossing Guadalupe Street: Growing Up Hispanic and Protestant, by David Maldonado, Jr. 2001001672. 082632231X pb. University of New Mexico, 2001. Mexican Americans, Protestants, Seguin, Texas.

Early Tejano Ranching: Daily Life at Ranchos San José & El Fresnillo by Andrés Sáenz. Edited by Andrés Tijerina. 2001033181. 1585441341 hc. 1585441635 pb. Texas A&M with University of Texas Institute of Texan Cultures, 1999, 2001. 186 pages, black-and-white photographs, 24 cm., index. Texas, Duval County, Mexican Americans, ranch life.

*Henry Cisneros: A Man of the People, by Maritza Romero. 97007431. 0823950824 lib. bdg. PowerKids, 1997. 24 pages, 19 x 20 cm., index. RL: 4.6, IL: K–3, grades 2–3. Accelerated Reader, Reading Counts. Cabinet officers, mayors, Mexican Americans, politicians, San Antonio, Texas.

The Making of a Chicano Militant: Lessons from Cristal, by José Ángel Gutierrez. *Wisconsin Studies in Autobiography* series. 98013866. 0299159809 hc. 0299159841 pb. University of Wisconsin, 1998. 368 pages, illustrated, map. Booklist. Crystal City, Texas, Mexican Americans, political activists.

Memorias, a West Texas Life, by Salvador Guerrero, edited by Arnoldo De León. 90023727. 0896722554 hc. Texas Tech University, 1991. 142 pages, illustrated, map. Mexican Americans, San Angelo, Texas, west Texas.

My Spanish-Speaking Left Foot, by José A. Cárdenas. 1878550597 pb. IDRA, 1997. 136 pages, 23 cm. Mexican Americans, Laredo, Texas, Mexico, education.

A Place in El Paso: A Mexican-American Childhood, by Gloria Lopez-Stafford. 95032451. 082631709X pb. University of New Mexico, 1996. 212 pages. El Paso, Texas, Mexican Americans.

Places Left Unfinished at the Time of Creation, by John Phillip Santos. 99013228. 0670868086 hc. 0140292020 pb. Viking, 1999. Penguin, 2000. 288 pages. *Booklist, Kirkus, Los Angeles Times, New York Times*. Mexican Americans, San Antonio, Texas.

¿Ya Será Hora? (Is It Time?), by Alejo Salinas, Jr. A. Salinas, 1998. 227 pages, 22 cm. Autobiography, Mexican Americans, Starr County, Texas, education, history.

▶ **977.3 Illinois**

Gabriel's Fire, by Luis Gabriel Aguilera. 99016610. 0226010678 hc. University of Chicago, 2000. 304 pages. *Booklist*. Chicago, Illinois, inner cities, Mexican Americans, youth.

▶ **978.9 New Mexico**

Low 'N Slow: Lowriding in New Mexico, by Carmella Padilla. Photographs by Jack Parsons. Poetry by Juan Estevan Arellano. 98031198. 0890133727 hc. 0890133735 pb. Museum of New Mexico Press, 1999. 120 pages, color illustrations, 32 cm. *Latina, Los Angeles Times*. Automobiles, lowriders, New Mexico.

They Called Me "King Tiger": My Struggle for the Land and Our Rights, by Reies López Tijerina. Translated and edited by José Ángel Gutierrez. *Hispanic Civil Rights* series. 00059426. 1558853022 pb. Arte, 2000. 224 pages. Civil rights, land tenure, Mexican Americans, New Mexico.

▶ **979.1 Arizona**

Images and Conversations: Mexican Americans Recall a Southwestern Past, by Patricia Preciado Martin, photographs by Louis Carlos Bernal. 83001186. 0816508038 pb. University of Arizona, 1983. 111 pages, black-and-white photographs, 22 x 26 cm. Mexican Americans, Tucson Region, Arizona.

▶ **979.4 California**

Days of Obligation: An Argument with My Mexican Father, by Richard Rodríguez. 92054077. 0140096221 pb. Viking, 1992. 230 pages. *The Book Report*. California, ethnic identity, Mexican Americans, Mexico.

*Dionicio Morales: A Life in Two Cultures, by Dionicio Morales. 97022160. 1558852190 pb. 0613179633 lib. bdg. Econo-Clad. Piñata Books, 1997. 199 pages, 22 cm. IL: young adult. Mexican American Opportunity Foundation, political activists, California.

Great Indians of California by Mariano Guadalupe Vallejo, Padre Francisco Palou, and H. H. Bancroft. Edited by Harry Knill. Bellerophon Books, 1999. 48 pages, black-and-white drawings, 28 cm. Translations from Spanish manuscripts. California—History, Indians.

Migrant Daughter: Coming of Age as a Mexican American Woman, by Frances Esquibel Tywoniak and Mario T. García. 99040594. 0520219147 hc. 052021955 pb. University of California, 2000. 321 pages, illustrated. Mexican American, college students, migrant agricultural laborers, New Mexico, University of California.

Stewing in the Melting Pot: The Memoir of a Real American, by Robert Sanabria. 2001028137. 1892123460 hc. Capital Books, 2001. 250 pages, 25 cm. Cultural assimilation, Los Angeles, California, Mexican Americans, orphans.

Tales of Mexican California: Cosas de California, by Señor Don Antonio Franco Coronel. Edited by Doyce B. Nunis, Jr. Ill. by Alan Archambault. Trans. by Diane de Avalle-Arco. Bellerophon, 1994. 104 pages, black-and-white illustrations, 29 cm. California.

► **980 Latin American History**

*Wars of Independence, by Richard Sanchez. *Hispanic Heritage* series, vol. 4. 9433364. 1562393340 lib. bdg. 1562393847 pb. Abdo, 1994. 32 pages, illustrated, 26 cm. Latin America—History, Mexican War, 1846-1848, United States—History—Civil War, 1861–1865.

Chapter 8

Resource Materials for Cultural Education

This chapter contains resource materials that are Latino-specific. While materials in this section were not written for young readers, some may be suitable for use with children and young adults. The author has selected these resource materials because they offer valuable insights into Latino cultures.

Materials include books, videotapes, and Web sites. Information provided in these materials may be useful for librarians selecting items to add to professional library collections for use by educators. Other materials will be useful for librarians seeking to meet the needs of library users by adding diversity to library collections. Some of these books and videotapes will offer a Latino perspective for parents, educators, and students working individually or in formal or informal groups.

Listed Web sites in this chapter provide an array of information on Latino cultures, history, higher education and scholarships, magazines and journals, awards, organizations, and more. Readers should be aware that the Internet is constantly evolving. Web sites frequently appear and disappear and occasionally change owners. Therefore Internet users should always check sites before recommending them to others.

Books:

All Pianos Have Keys and Other Stories, by José A. Cárdenas. 1878550535 pb. Intercultural Development Research Association, 1994. 126 pages, 23 cm. Autobiographical stories from a veteran activist and educator of more than 50 years.

The Best of Latino Heritage: A Guide to the Best Juvenile Books about Latino People and Cultures, by Isabel Schon. Scarecrow Press, 1997. 96024249. 0810832216 hc. 285 pages, 23 cm., indexes. Critical analyses of a number of books by Latino authors and others.

Chicana/o Studies Paradigms: A Journal of Alternative Voices. Special issue: "Chicana/o Studies: An Academic Odyssey" Edited by Randall C. Jimenez and Marie C. Chin. Historical Science Publishing, 2000. Volume 1, No. 1. 233 pages, 22 cm. Articles by Latino professors on the history and status of California Chicana/o studies.

Hearts and Hands: Making Peace in a Violent Time, by Luis J. Rodríguez. Seven Stories Press, 2001. 2001041072. 1583222634 hc. 352 pages, 24 cm. Rodríguez writes of his own experiences, offers ideas for dealing with youth violence, and provides specific strategies for change.

Hispanic Families as Valued Partners: An Educator's Guide, by María Robledo Montecel and others.1878550470 pb. Intercultural Development Research Association, 1993. 59 pages, illustrated, 23 x 32 cm., bibliographies, resource lists. Information on Hispanic students and families in the United States.

Indo-Hispanic Folk Art Traditions I: Christmas and Other Year-Round Activities = Tradiciones artesanales indo-hispanas I: Navidad y otras activides para todo el año, by Bobbi Salinas. Piñata Publications, 1987. 0934925038 pb. 165 pages, illus. 29 cm. Bilingual text. Information about traditions and instructions for costumes. Includes posadas, piñatas, dough art, luminarias/farolitos, yarn painting, recipes, and more.

Indo-Hispanic Folk Art Traditions II: Day of the Dead = Tradiciones artesanales indo-hispanas II: Día de los muertos, by Bobbi Salinas. Piñata Publications, 1988. 934925046 pb. Bilingual text. Comparable to Volume I with emphasis on the Day of the Dead.

Keep Blessing Us, Ultima: A Teaching Guide for Bless Me, Ultima, by Abelardo Baeza. Eakin Press, 1997. 97163113. 1571681582 pb. 67 pages, illustrated, 23 cm. Activities, tests, author profile, essay and project topics, glossary, selected bibliography.

Navidad latinoamericana = Latin American Christmas, by Charito Calvachi Wakefield. Latin American Creations Publishing, 1999. 0966069013 hc. Third edition. book + compact disc. 88 pages, color illustrations, 23 cm. Sound disc contains two versions of 12 Latin American Christmas carols on 24 tracks. All songs are in Spanish. Traditional and folkloric versions of each song. Spanish and English lyrics in text. Text includes nine days of prayers for pre-Christmas religious observations and Christmas traditions from 25 Latin American countries.

Raising Nuestros Niños: Bringing Up Latino Children in a Bicultural World, by Gloria Rodríguez. Fireside, 1999. 2001273062. 0684839695 pb. 378 pages, bibliography, index.

Criando a nuestros niños: educando a niños latinos en un mundo bicultural. Simon & Schuster, 1999. 2001368506. 0684841266 pb. 411 pages, bibliography, index. Teaching Hispanic children who they are: background, future, developmental needs, effective parenting. Lists support groups, books and cassettes.

Recommended Books in Spanish for Children and Young Adults, 1996 through 1999, by Isabel Schon. Scarecrow Press, 2000. 00038761. 0810838400 hc. 376 pages, indexes. Critical analyses of books in Spanish. Includes titles translated from English and non-Latino authors. An earlier volume covers 1991-1995.

Since My Brother Died = Desde Que Murió Mi Hermano, by Marisol Muñoz-Kiehne. Illustrated by Glenda Dietrich. Centering Corporation, 2000. 00045199. 1561231355 pb. 20 pages, color illustrations, 18 x 23 cm. English and Spanish text on single pages. Grieving from a child's point of view; notes to parents, teachers, and counselors.

U. S. Latino Literature: A Critical Guide for Students and Teachers, edited by Harold Augenbraum and Margarite Fernández Olmos. Greenwood Press, 2000. 99462065. 0313311374 hc. 230 pages. 25 cm. *School Library Journal*. Eighteen chapters by authoritative authors on Latino writers. Bibliographies. Sample course outline, gay and lesbian authors, Web resources, areas for independent study.

Videotapes:

Brown and Black and White All Over. Antonio Sacre and Jenny Magnus. Chicago: Curious Theater Branch. Age 17 & up. 70-minute videotape.

Heart of the Imaginero: Little Wood Carver. Edwin Fontánez. Exit Studio, 2000. 60-minute videotape. English narration. For all ages. Magical story of Eduardito who becomes a carver of santos (saints).

The Legend of the Vejigante Make-a-Mask Video and Activity Book Set. Exit Studio, 1994. *The Vejigante & the Folk Festivals of Puerto Rico* book, by Edwin Fontánez. 0964086808 pb. 36 pages, illustrated. Video 20 minutes, English language. Bilingual mask-making guide. Package contains video, activity book, and pack of crayons. Ages 8+.

Taino: The Activity Book and Video Set, by Edwin Fontánez. Exit Studio, 1996. 0964086832 pb. Book 44 pages, illustrations. Video 25 minutes. Ages 8+. Puerto Rico before the Spanish Conquest. Includes historical notes and glossary for parents or teachers. Video packaged with activity book and pack of crayons. Spanish or English.

Tapestry II. Rosa Guerrero. Carlos F. Ortega. University of Texas at El Paso. Focuses on the life and career of veteran educator Rosa Guerrero, who is Artist-in-Residence at UTEP. <www.utep.edu/chicano/Grosa.htm>

Tribes and Bridges. Storytellers Antonio Sacre, La'Ron Williams, and Susan O'Halloran. Sponsored by Angels Studio. Age 12 & up. 120 minutes. <www.racebridges.net>

Validating the Student's Culture in the Classroom. Henry Stewart of Louisiana Public Broadcasting and Dr. Frank Gonzales of the Intercultural Development Research Association, 1991. 30 minutes. Discusses the need for teachers to validate and value the cultures of all students in the classroom. Discusses surface culture and deep culture.

Web Sites:

American G. I. Forum
Américas Award <www.uwm.edu/Dept/CLACS/outreach_americas.html>
ASPIRA
Boricua.com
Bronze Pages <http://clnet.ucr.edu/people/people.html>
Centro de estudios puertorriqueños
Chi Chi Rodríguez Foundation <www.chichi.org/features/features_main.htm>
Chicano Latino Net <http://latino.sscnet.ucla.edu>
Congressional Hispanic Caucus <www.house.gov/reyes/CHC/Welcome.html>
Coqui.net (Puerto Rico)
Cuban American National Council
Cuban Committee for Democracy <www.us.net/cuban/>
¡del Corazón! <http://nmaa-ryder.si.edu/webzine/index.html>
Diversity Training University International <www.diversityuintl.com>
Dominican Studies Institute <www.ccny.cuny.edu/dominican/index.html>
Estela and Raúl Mora Award <www.ala.org/news/v7n4/mora_award.html>
Famous Hispanics <http://coloquio.com/famosos/alpha.html>
Hispanic.com
Hispanic America USA <www.neta.com/~1stbooks/index.html>
Hispanic Association of Colleges & Universities
Hispanic Heritage Posters <www.hmsdc.com/hispanic/index.htm>
Hispanic Journal
Hispanic Magazine <www.hispanicmagazine.com/subscribe/>
Hispanic Scholarship Fund <www.hsf.net/index.php>
Hispanic Times
Hispanic Writers Collection <www.library.swt.edu/swwc/misc/hispanic.html>
Hispanic Yearbook/Anuario Hispano <www.tiym.com/anuai.htm>
Hispanics in America's Defense <www.neta.com/~1stbooks/defense.htm>
Hopscotch magazine <http://muse.jhu.edu/journals/hop/>
Ideas! and Curriculum Extension <www.patmora.com/ideas.htm>
Imagen: la voz latina magazine
Institute of Texan Cultures <www.texancultures.utsa.edu/public/index.htm>
Intercultural Development Research Association <www.idra.org>
Inter-University Program for Latino Research <www.nd.edu/%7Eiuplr/>
Journal of Latinos & Education <www.erlbaum.com/Journals/journals/JLE/jle.htm>
Julian Samora Research Institute
Latina magazine

Latino Issues Forum <www.lif.org/>

Latino USA: The Radio Journal of News and Culture <www.latinousa.org/>

League of United Latin American Citizens <www.lulac.org/Index.html>

Library of Congress Hispanic Reading Room <http://lcweb.loc.gov/rr/hispanic/>

LibrUsa <www.librusa.com>

MANA: A National Latina Organization <www.hermana.org/>

El Mesteño Magazine <www.el-mesteno.com>

Mexican American Legal Defense and Education Fund <www.maldef.org/>

las mujeres <www.lasmujeres.com/>

National Alliance for Hispanic Health <www.hispanichealth.org/>

National Council of La Raza <www.nclr.org/>

National Hispana Leadership Institute <www.nhli.org/>

National Hispanic Environmental Council <www.nheec.org>

National Latino Children's Institute <www.nlci.org>

Nosotros <www.nosotros.org/>

Online ESL Links <www.geocities.com/Athens/Academy/4843/onlineesl.htm>

Puerto Rican Web Sites <www.puertorican.org/>

Pura Belpré Award <www.ala/org/alsc/belpre.html>

Raza Review <www.razareview.com>

Recommended Latino Web Sites <www.public.iastate.edu/~savega/us_latin.htm>

REFORMA <www.reforma.org/>

Saludos Hispanos <www.saludos.com/>

Smithsonian Center for Latino Initiatives <http://latino.si.edu/>

Spanish Culture <http://spanishculture.about.com>

Taco Shop Poets <http://tacoshoppoets.org>

Teaching Tolerance <www.tolerance.org/teach/index.jsp>

Tomás Rivera Award <www.education.swt.edu/rivera/mainpage.html>

Tomás Rivera Policy Institute <www.trpi.org/>

Vista Magazine <www.vistamagazine.com/>

Chapter 9

Latino Writers of Children's and Young Adult Literature

Most information in the following section is taken from book jackets and covers or interior book pages containing author information. Readers may assume that the source of each biography is a book by that author unless another source is indicated. Although some of these authors are listed in *Something About the Author*, *Dictionary of American Biography*, *Authors and Artists for Young Adults*, or other biographical reference books, those resources were not used for these brief biographies.

Some information has been taken from Web sites. If no Web site is listed for an author, that indicates that no Web site is currently available. However, new sites are being added frequently, so additional sites may appear. Whenever possible, official Web sites have been listed; however, some sites represent commercial publishers. When a variety of Web sites existed, an effort was made to locate and select the most useful sites.

Web sites listed were accurate at the time of publication. However, readers should be aware that changes may occur when a domain name shifts ownership. Therefore, those planning to suggest these sites to others should first check the listed sites to be sure they still contain appropriate content.

Only authors of books listed in this guide have been included in this chapter. Translators and illustrators are not listed. Chapter 10 contains the names of Latino writers who have written for general or adult audiences.

María Armengol Acierno is the author of *The Children of Flight Pedro Pan*.

Alma Flor Ada was born in Cuba. Ada has published a number of books of fiction as well as two autobiographical works in Mexico, Spain, and Peru as well as the United States. She is a professor of multicultural education in San Francisco, California.

Luis Gabriel Aguilera is the cofounder of a musical production company. He grew up in Chicago where he now lives.
<www.press.uchicago.edu/cgi-bin/hfs.cgi/00/13916.ctl>

Julia Alvarez is originally from the Dominican Republic. Her family immigrated to the United States when she was ten. She is the author of several books for adults and a picture book. Alvarez is writer-in-residence at Middlebury College.
<http://voices.cla.umn.edu/authors/JuliaAlvarez.html>
<www.emory.edu/ENGLISH/Bahri/Alvarez.html>

Adela Amador is a native New Mexican. She is the author of several books that combine cookery and her New Mexican culture.
<http://amadorbooks.com/authaa.htm>

Rudolfo Anaya is a native of New Mexico and the author of *Bless Me, Ultima*, a classic of Mexican-American literature. He has written numerous books, including mysteries, fiction, children's books, and picture books. Anaya lives in Albuquerque.
<http://web.nmsu.edu/~tomlynch/swlit.anaya.html>
<www.unm.edu/~wrtgsw/anaya.html>

George Ancona is an author, photographer, and illustrator of many nonfiction books. Originally from Brooklyn, he now lives with his family in Santa Fe, New Mexico.
<http://teacher.scholastic.com/authorsndbooks/authors/ancona.bio.htm>
<www.eduplace.com/kids/hmr/mtai/ancona.html>

Zoë Anglesey has taught in a prison, high schools, and colleges in New York City and Washington. She has conducted poetry workshops in Seattle and has edited magazines.
<www.randomhouse.com/catalog/display.pperl?isbn=0345428978#bio>

Marie Arana grew up in Peru. Her father was Peruvian and her mother American. Arana is editor of *The Washington Post Book World* and lives in Washington, D.C.
<www.randomhouse.com/bantamdell/catalog/display.pperl?isbn=0385319622#bio>

Juan Estevan Arellano is a magazine publisher and writer and is the director of the Oñate Cultural Center in New Mexico.

<www.nmcn.org/artsorgs/writersguide/arellano.html>

Alfred Avila (1933–2001) was the author of *Mexican Ghost Tales of the Southwest*. He was a resident of California and a Navy veteran.

<http://ussmontrose.homestead.com/Fifties.html>

<www.geocities.com/buscandocalifornia/folk/alfr.html>

<www.geocities.com/buscandocalifornia/folk/mexi.html>

Kat Avila is the editor of *Mexican Ghost Tales of the Southwest*, which features her father's stories. She lives in California.

<www.jademagazine.com/5iss_dumbq.html>

Jimmy Santiago Baca is a native New Mexican poet. Baca grew up in the Albuquerque area and endured a difficult childhood. After time spent in prison, he found within himself a poet's soul. The author of several books of poetry and memoirs, this poet also has produced and directed a video movie.

<www.swcp.com/~baca/biography.html>

<http://web.nmsu.edu/~tomlynch/swlit.baca.html>

Abelardo Baeza, Ph.D. is a native of Alpine, Texas. He is a professor of English and Spanish and director of Mexican American Studies at Sul Ross State University in Alpine. Baeza's writing includes numerous Spanish-language plays, newspaper and journal articles, a teaching guide, and a biography.

<www.sulross.edu/~langlit/baeza.html>

Kathy Balmes is the author of *Thunder on the Sierra*. She lives in Marin County, California with her husband and two daughters.

Marietta Barrón grew up in mining camps of the western United States. She lived and worked in Beverly Hills. A retired teacher of multicultural children, she wishes to tell the story of poverty and prejudice that she remembers. Barrón now lives in Carmichael, California.

Pura Belpré was an Afro-Puerto Rican librarian at the New York Public Library. Also a storyteller and writer, she wrote several children's books during her lifetime (1899–1982). A major literary award honors Pura Belpré.

<www.reforma.org/belpre.html>

<http://bluehawk.monmouth.edu/~lromeo/newbery/sld008.htm>

Roy P. Benavidez (1935–1998) was a decorated soldier in Vietnam and was awarded a Medal of Honor. Despite painful disabilities, Benavidez spent the last years of his life working with young people to encourage patriotism and prevent drug abuse.
<www.mishalov.com/Benavidez.html>
<http://carrasco.home.texas.net/roy-obit.htm>
<www.geocities.com/Pentagon/Quarters/8061/tribute.html>

Anilú Bernardo has written several books for young adults. She is originally from Santiago, Cuba. She and her family immigrated to the United States in 1961. Bernardo now lives with her husband and two daughters in Florida.
<www.popano.net/~anilu/>

Carmen T. Bernier-Grand grew up in Puerto Rico and taught mathematics at the University of Puerto Rico before she moved to the mainland. She worked as a librarian until she began to write as a full-time career. She and her family now live in Portland, Oregon.
<www.cynthialeitichsmith.com/auth-illCarmenTBernierGrand.htm>

Diane Gonzales Bertrand is the author of several picture books as well as children's and young adult fiction. The mother of two, Bertrand lives and works in her hometown, San Antonio, Texas.
<www.childrenslit.com/f_dianegonzales.html>

Geoff Boucher is originally from Florida. He began writing for United Press International when he was seventeen. Boucher is now a reporter for the *Los Angeles Times*, specializing in street gangs.

Sue Boulais is a freelance editor and writer living in Orlando, Florida. Boulais is the author of several books and has worked as an editor for *Weekly Reader*.
<www.eduplace.com/kids/hmr/mtai/boulais.html>

José Antonio Burciaga (1940–1996) was a talented artist and writer. He published several works of essays and poetry before his untimely death. Burciaga was a founding member of Culture Clash.
<www.stanford.edu/group/SCCR/Burciaga.html>

Ramiro Burr is a music journalist for the *San Antonio Express News*. He is the author of a syndicated column that appears weekly in several newspapers in Texas. Burr also is a regular contributor to national magazines.

Viola Canales is a native of McAllen, Texas. A graduate of Harvard College and Harvard Law School, she was a captain in the U.S. Army. She was appointed to the U.S. Small Business Administration by President Clinton in 1994. Canales lives in California.

Hector Cantú and **Carlos Castellanos** are co-authors of the comic strip *Baldo*. Cantú, a journalist, has written for several newspapers and now lives in Texas with his wife and three children. Castellanos has done illustrations for magazines, books, and corporate clients. He lives in Florida with his wife and two children.
<www.baldocomics.com>

José A. Cárdenas, Ed.D. was born in Laredo, Texas. He founded the Intercultural Development Research Association (IDRA) in 1973 and served as director until his retirement in 1992. Cárdenas is the author of several books on multicultural education and school finance.
<www.idra.org/WhosWho/IDRAStaff.htm#José_Cárdenas>

Lori Marie Carlson has edited and translated several award-winning anthologies of Latino literature. She lives in New York City.
<www.harpercollins.com/catalog/author_xml.asp?authorID=15263>

Julia Mercedes Castilla is originally from Bogota, Colombia. The author of several books in English and in Spanish, she lives in Houston, Texas.
<www.scbwi-houston.org/Julia%20Castilla.htm>

Rafaela G. Castro worked as a librarian at several universities in Oregon and California. She also has been a lecturer at the University of California at Berkeley.
<http://sb1.abc-clio.com:81/>

Veronica Chambers, executive editor at *Savoy Magazine*, is the author of fiction and nonfiction for children and teens. She has been published in *New York Times Magazine*, *Vogue*, *Elle, Essence, Glamour, Redbook,* and *Seventeen.* Chambers lives in New York.
<www.findarticles.com/m1264/3_31/63165478/pl/article.jhtml>
<www.pen.org/readers/sites/nyc/vcvisit.html>
<http://arts.endow.gov/explor/Writers/Chambers.html>

Jesús Colón (1901–1974) was a Puerto Rican journalist. His writings represent a historical Puerto Rican viewpoint.
<http://oak.cats.ohiou.edu/~rouzie/569A/benington/bios.htm>

Rosa Coronado grew up in Minnesota where her parents operated a restaurant, La Casa Coronado. After high school she attended the University of Mexico in Mexico City.

Coronado has worked as a restaurateur and has taught in a cooking school. In 1975, she was the first woman admitted to the Geneva Executive Chefs Association, an international organization of food specialists and chefs.

John R. Craig is a co-author of Roy Benavidez's *Medal of Honor* and several other books.

Bárbara C. Cruz, Ed.D. is a professor at the University of South Florida in Tampa. Cruz is the author of several biographies and other books on current issues.
<http://ldap.acomp.usf.edu/directory/email_search.php>

Diane de Anda, Ph.D. is the author of a picture book, short story books, and nonfiction. A professor in the Department of Social Welfare at the University of California at Los Angeles, de Anda has worked as a community worker and teacher. The mother of two, she lives with her husband in Los Angeles.
<www.sppsr.ucla.edu/faculty/webpage.cfm?lastname=deAnda&vita_online=NO>

Diane de Avalle-Arce is a freelance translator, reviewer, and magazine editor. She lives in Santa Barbara, California.
<www.dawnwich.com/Avesta/VQ/arce.html>

Beatriz De La Garza, author of books of short stories as well as a novel, is a lawyer and has served as president of the board of the Austin Independent School District in Austin, Texas.

Arnoldo De León, Ph.D. is a professor of history at Angelo State University in San Angelo, Texas. He is a member of the Texas State Historical Association and is the author of several nonfiction books on Mexican Americans in Texas.
<www.angelo.edu/directory/faculty_staff/deleon_dr_arnoldo.html>

Lulu Delacre's parents were from Argentina. She grew up in Puerto Rico. Delacre has received several awards for children's books she has written and illustrated. She lives with her husband and daughters in Maryland.
<www.childrensbookguild.org/luludelacre.html>
<http://teacher.scholastic.com/authorsandbooks/authors/delacre/bio.htm>

Miguel Durán is a counselor for youth gangs. *Don't Spit on My Corner* is based on his experiences as a teenage pachuco during the World War II era.

Susan Dworkin is a playwright and journalist. She is a co-author of *The Ms. Guide to a Woman's Health* and *Lost in the System*.

Flor Fernandez-Barrios was born in Cuba. She came to the United States in 1970 when she was fourteen and now lives in Seattle, Washington.
<www.alibi.com/alibi/1999-09-02/speeder.html>
<http://seattletimes.mwsource.com/news/entertainment/html98/thun_19991202.html>

Carlos M. Fernández-Shaw has served as a diplomat in embassies in Italy, Canada, Paraguay, Sweden, and Denmark. His career also has included work as a cultural attaché, consul general, and ambassador to several countries. In addition, he is a lawyer, writer, and historian.

Sergio Flores is the author of *Good Morning Alberto*.

Camille Flores-Turney has worked as a journalist for *New Mexico Magazine* and the *Albuquerque Journal*. She has worked as an editor with several business magazines and continues as a freelance writer.

Edwin Fontánez is an author, artist, and film maker. He has presented cultural awareness workshops for children in Washington, D.C. Fontanez is founder of Exit Studio, which produces educational materials on Puerto Rican culture and history.
<www.exitstudio.com/html/exitstud.htm>

Ernesto Galarza (1905–1984) was a pioneer Mexican-American writer. He was born in Mexico and came with his family to California. *Barrio Boy* is the story of his early life.
<www.chass.ucr.edu/csbsr/gala.htm>
<www.stanford.edu/group/SCCR/galarza.html>

Rudy Galindo is a professional skater. He has been featured on a Tour of World Figure Skating Champions and competes in many televised competitions. Galindo lives in San Jose, California.
<www.southam.com/skating/galindo1.html>

José Gálvez is a photojournalist. He was lead photographer of the *L.A. Times* team that received a Pulitzer Prize for its portrayal of Latinos in Southern California. He lives with his wife in Tucson, Arizona.

Harry Gamboa, Jr. is an artist whose works have been exhibited at the Museum of Modern Art in New York, the Smithsonian Institution, and others. Gamboa lives in Los Angeles.
<www.oversight.com/chicanoville/TEXT/biography/index.html>

John García is the author of *The Success of Hispanic Magazine*. He has worked as a journalist.
<http://abclocal.go.com/wls/aboutus/wls_bio_JohnGarcia.html>

Kimberly García is a bilingual journalist. She worked for six years as a daily newspaper journalist in Texas and Wisconsin. Her writings have appeared in *Hispanic, Vista*, and *Latina* magazines. García lives in Austin, Texas.

Lionel G. García combines the careers of writer and veterinarian. He has written several books of fiction, biographical works, and a picture book. *Hardscrub* received the Texas Institute of Letters Novel of the Year Award and several other awards in 1990.
<www.707.vwh1.net/wisd12/Mission.html>

Mario T. García is a professor at the University of California, Santa Barbara. He has written and edited several award-winning books.
<http://research.ucsb.edu/ccs/peop.htm#Mario>

Juanita Garciagodoy is a teacher in the Spanish Department at Macalester College in St. Paul, Minnesota.
<www.macalester.edu/~spanish/faculty.html>

Hedda Garza (1929–1995) was a lecturer, editor, and freelance writer. Her articles on Hispanic culture and history were published in several magazines and newspapers. Garza was the author of several books for young adults as well as other scholarly works.

Albino Gonzales is a native of New Mexico. He grew up in a rural setting with strong ties to his grandparents and other family members.

Doreen Gonzales worked as a teacher before becoming a full-time writer. She has published several nonfiction books. Gonzales likes to camp, hike, and ski with her family.

Lucia M. González was born in Cuba. She is the author of several books for children.
<www.eduplace.com/kids/hmr/mtai/gonzalez.html>

Ray González is a well-known poet and is editor of a number of excellent anthologies containing works of Latino poets and writers.
<www.barriolife.com/stories/rattlerdreams.html>

Christine Granados has worked as a newspaper reporter, editor, and writer. She was editor of *Moderna* magazine and reporter for the *Long Beach Press-Telegram*, *The El Paso Times*, and the *Austin American-Statesman*. Her feature stories have appeared in numerous magazines.

Salvador Guerrero grew up in San Angelo, Texas, where he attended junior college. Guerrero served in World War II and settled in Odessa, Texas where he worked in broadcasting and in politics.

<www.oaoa.com/twentieth/cent_salguerrero.htm>

José Ángel Gutierrez was a co-founder of La Raza Unida, an activist political party in the early 1970s. A native of Crystal City, Texas, he became president of the school board in that town and later earned his law degree.

<www.uta.edu/cgi-bin/X500/staff2.pl>

<http://hrcweb.utsa.edu/test/jose_angel_gutierrez_collection.htm>

Lila Guzmán is the author of *Green Slime and Jam* and *Green Slime and Sushi* in addition to *Lorenzo's Secret Mission*. She also publishes an e-newsletter for novice writers.

<http://home.austin.rr.com/asktheauthor/>

Rick Guzmán is an attorney and the co-author of a book of historical fiction. He lives with his family in Round Rock, Texas.

<http://home.austin.rr.com/asktheauthor/>

George Hadley-García is the author of *Hollywood Hispano/Hispanic Hollywood*.

Elva Treviño Hart was born in south Texas. Her parents were migrant farm workers. She attended school in Pearsall, Texas and earned degrees in theoretical mathematics and computer science engineering at Stanford University. Hart worked in the computer field and now lives in Virginia.

<www.ci.austin.tx.us/library/071999.htm>

Gerald Haslam is Professor Emeritus at Sonoma State University. He has been recognized with a number of awards, including Josephine Miles and Benjamin Franklin Awards. He is the father of Garth Haslam and four other children.

<www.sonic.net/~ghaslam/booklist.htm>

Janice Haslam teaches at St. Vincent de Paul High School in Petaluma, California. *Manuel and the Madman* is the result of her first collaboration with Gerald Haslam.

Irene Beltrán Hernández worked as a caseworker with Adolescent Services in Dallas, Texas before retirement. She is the author of three novels for young adults. Hernández lives in Satin, Texas.

Jo Ann Yolanda Hernández, a native of Texas, has published short stories in several journals. *White Bread Competition* is her first book.
<www.bronzeword.com/About%20the%20Author.htm>

Juan Felipe Herrera is a professor at California State University. He is the author of several picture books and books of poetry for children and young adults. He lives with his family in Fresno, California.
<www.corona.bell.k12.ca.us/comm/juan.html>
<www.loc.gov/today/pr/2000/00-083.html>

Oscar Hijuelos is a Cuban-American writer, a Pulitzer Prize winner, and a New Yorker.
<www.fdu.edu/newspubs/pressrel/hijuelos.html>
<www.harpercollins.com/catalog/author_xml.asp?authorID=4476>

María Hinojosa is a National Public Radio correspondent. She is host of the NPR program, *Latino U.S.A.* Hinojosa is also a panelist on two television talk shows in New York.
<www.cnn.com/CNN/anchors_reporters/hinojosa.maria.html>
<www.utexas.edu/admin/opa/news/99newsreleases/nr_199907/nr_latino990708.html>

Francisco Jiménez has written several picture books and novels based on his migrant worker childhood. He is a professor of modern languages at Santa Clara University in California.
<www.scu.edu/SCU/Programs/Diversity/panch.html>

Kevin Johnson is a professor of law at the University of California, Davis. Because of his Anglo surname, Johnson has a special viewpoint on being Latino.
<www.ocis.temple.edu/tempress/titles/1398_reg.html>
<www.pubcomm.ucdavis.edu/newsreleases/04.99/news_kevinjohnson.html>

Nicolás Kanellos, Ph.D. is an author and founder of Arte Público Press in Houston, Texas. Kanellos is of Puerto Rican descent and is a strong proponent of Latino literature.
<www.uh.edu/ia/farfel/Kan.html>
<www.oup-usa.org/isbn/019513527X.html#author>

Graciela Kenig is a columnist for *¡Exito!*, a Spanish-language newspaper published by the *Chicago Tribune*. Her field is jobs and careers, and Kenig has interviewed numerous Latinos who bring the richness of their Latino heritage to their careers.
<www.diversityspeakers.com/speakers/Graciela_Kenig.html>

Ofelia Dumas Lachtman is the author of several novels and picture books for children and young adults. She lives in California.

<www.eduplace.com/kids/hmr/mtai/lachtman.html>

<www.childrenslit.com/f_ofelialachtman.html>

Carmen Lizardi-Rivera is a college professor and translator.

<www.sjsu.edu/depts/foreign_lang/faculty/facultytext.html#carmen>

<www.sjsu.edu/depts/foreign_lang/sp/lizardihome.html>

Carmen Lomas Garza is an artist whose picture books have won a number of awards. Originally from south Texas, Lomas Garza now lives and works in San Francisco. Her works of art, which express pride in her Mexican-American culture, have been exhibited in many galleries and museums.

<www.tfaoi.com/aa/2aa/2aa436.htm>

<http://mati.eas.asu.edu:8421/ChicanArte/html_pages/CamenIssOutl.html#artmaker>

Mario Longoria attended universities in California and Texas. He is a Vietnam veteran, a researcher and writer, and a training specialist for an insurance company in San Antonio, Texas.

<http://mati.eas.asu.edu:8421/bilingual/HTML/athletes.html>

Charlotte Lopez is a former Miss Teen USA and is the author of *Lost in the System*. She attended the University of California at Irvine.

Elena López is a co-author of *The Story of Mexico*.

Gloria Lopez-Stafford grew up in El Paso, Texas. She has published an outstanding memoir about her childhood as the daughter of an Anglo man and a Mexican women.

Olga Loya is a storyteller and a writer. She has told stories in schools, museums, and festivals across the United States and Mexico. Loya lives in San Jose, California.

<www.augusthouse.com/0-87483-580-1.htm>

Antonio Hernández Madrigal grew up in Mexico. He came to the United States in 1976 and has worked at many jobs. He has written several children's books and picture books.

<www.fulcrum-resources.com/html/madrigal.html>

David Maldonado, Jr. grew up in Seguin, Texas. Maldonado is president of a school of theology in Denver, Colorado.

<www.iliff.edu/about_iliff/faculty_davidm.htm>

Eric Marcus is a writer and has worked in television.
<www.ericmarcus.com/bio.htm>

Christine Marin is the curator and archivist of the Chicano Research Collection at the Hayden Library of Arizona State University, Tempe. She is a teacher, writer, and editor.
<www.asu.edu/lib/archives/damstaff.htm>

George Mariscal is a professor of literature at the University of California, San Diego. He is an author, editor, and Vietnam veteran.
<www.ucpress.edu/books/pages/8184.html#bio>

Herón Márquez was born in Mexico and moved to California when he was six. He had a short career in semiprofessional baseball before working as a journalist and writer for various newspapers. Márquez and his wife live in St. Paul, Minnesota.

Patricia Preciado Martin, a native of Arizona, is a lifelong resident of Tucson, where she has been active in collecting oral history, writing, and developing the Mexican Heritage Project at the Arizona Historical Society. She is the author of four books of fiction, short stories, and nonfiction.
<www.deserthawkbooks.com/daysofplenty.html>
<www.uapress.arizona.edu/books/bid286.htm>

Elizabeth (Betita) Sutherland Martinez is a Chicana activist. She is the author of six books, has worked as a teacher, and works with youth and community groups. Martinez lives in San Francisco, California.
<www.infoshop.org/texts/crass_martinez.html>

Elizabeth Coonrod Martinez grew up in Mexico. She moved to the United States when she was seventeen. Martinez has worked as a journalist, translator, and writer. She lives in New Mexico.
<www.sonoma.edu/people/M/Martinez/>
<http://csumb.edu/workshops/media_humanities/participants/sonoma.html>

Floyd Martinez, Ph.D. works in community mental health in Portland, Oregon. He is a New Mexico native, and *Spirits of the High Mesa* was his first novel.

Soraida Martinez is a Puerto Rican artist. She was born in New York City. Her art provides insight into her concern with the issues of sexism, racism, and stereotyping.
<www.soraida.com>.

Victor Martinez grew up in Fresno, California. He has worked as a farm worker, truck driver, firefighter, and teacher. He has published poetry and short stories. *Parrot in the Oven*, his first novel, has earned a number of prestigious awards.
<www.harperchildrens.com/rgg/rggparrot.htm>
<www.pbs.org/newshour/bb/entertainment/november96/martinez_11-7.html>

Valerie Menard was managing editor of *La Prensa*, a biweekly publication, until 1994 when she became an editor of *Hispanic Magazine*. An advocate for Latinos, Menard is the author of several biographies.

Patrick M. Mendoza is a storyteller, musician, singer, and writer. He has written several books on Native Americans. Of Cuban ancestry, Mendoza's family moved from Florida to Denver when he was eight.
<www.augusthouse.com/pmendoza.htm>
<http://hometown.aol.com/patmendoza/patbio.html>

Vincent L. Mendoza is the author of *Son of Two Bloods*. Mendoza, a native of Oklahoma, is a Vietnam veteran.
<http://ipl.si.umich.edu/cgi/ref/native/browse.pl/A404>

Brigid Aileen Milligan is the daughter of Bryce and Mary Guerrero Milligan. She attended school in San Antonio, Texas, and has been writing since she was very young. A National Hispanic Scholar, Brigid also has been recognized for her work in science and engineering and has received prizes for her poetry, plays, and videos. She is now attending college.
<www.wingspress.com/Titles/brigid.html>

Nicholasa Mohr was born in New York City and has received several prestigious awards for her writing. She lives in New York.
<http://voices.cla.umn.edu/authors/NicholasaMohr.html>
<http://teacher.scholastic.com/authorsandbooks/events/mohr/bio.htm>

Manuel Monterrey is a photojournalist. He has worked with the Associated Press and with newspapers.
<www.twbookmark.com/authors/8/1592/index.html>

Marisa Montes was born in Puerto Rico and traveled with her military family as a child. As a lawyer, she edited and wrote law books before she began writing for children. She and her husband live in northern California.
<www.harpercollins.com/catalog/author_xml.asp?authorID=14980>

Pat Mora is a poet and author of numerous picture books. The mother of three, this El Paso native divides her time between New Mexico and Kentucky.
<http://voices.cla.umn.edu/authors/patmora.html>

Dionicio Morales was born October 9, 1918 in Arizona. Morales is the founder of the Mexican American Opportunity Foundation in Ventura County, California.

Alice Morin is the author of more than 30 plays. She teaches in the Palm Springs, California where she works with students in English-language programs and drama.
<http://members.aol.com/normorin/3plays3.htm>

Carlos Morton, Ph.D. is a playwright and professor at the University of California, Riverside.
<www.theatre.ucr.edu/people/morton.html>

Alma Muñoz Maya is a co-author of *Madonas de/of Mexico*.

Yolanda Nava works as a newspaper and television journalist, educator and consultant, and community leader in California.
<www.chocolateforwomen.com/contributors/N.htm>
<www.simonsays.com/author.cfm?isbn=0684849003>

Ruben Navarrette, Jr. graduated from Harvard University in 1990. His writing has been published in the *Arizona Republic*, the *San Francisco Chronicle, Hispanic*, and several other newspapers and magazines.
<www.postwritersgroup.com/bionava.htm>

Donna Neary is a co-author of *The Story of Mexico* from Bellerophon Books.

Chon A. Noriega is a professor at the University of California, Los Angeles. Noriega has edited several works on Latinos in film.
<www.tft.ucla.edu/Faculty/faccrit.htm>

Himilce Novas has written for the *New York Times, Christian Science Monitor, Cuisine*, and other periodicals. She is the author of a number of books and is the host of a radio show.
<www.penguinputnam.com/Author/AuthorFrame/0,1018,,00.html?0CS^0000019196_BIO>
<www.wingsbooks.com/catalog/display.pperl?isbn=0679444084#bio>

Doyce B. Nunis, Jr. edited *Tales of Mexican California* for Bellerophon Books.

George Ochoa is the author of several reference books and books for young adults.

Edward James Olmos is an actor and producer. Olmos is also an activist and frequently speaks at schools, charities, and juvenile institutions around the country.
<www.kepplerassociates.com/olmos.htm>
<http://classics.www5.50megs.com/vice/ejolmos.htm>

Yvonne Ortiz, a culinary professional, grew up in Cayey, Puerto Rico. She has published frequently in *El Diario/La Prensa, Gourmet*, and the *New York Times*.

Judith Ortiz Cofer was born in Puerto Rico. She has written numerous books that have received prestigious awards. Ortiz Cofer is a professor at the University of Georgia in Athens.
<www.albany.edu/writers-inst/cofer.html>
<http://parallel.park.uga.edu/~jcofer/>

Valerie Ozeta grew up in California and has traveled extensively. Ozeta has a degree in telecommunications and film and has worked on films such as "Mi Familia" and in plays. She now teaches in Pacoima, California.
<www.gotwolf.com/index.html>

Carmella Padilla edited *Low 'N Slow* for the Museum of New Mexico Press.

Américo Paredes (1915-1999) was born in Brownsville, Texas. He attended the University of Texas at Austin where he taught for many years and was active in researching the folklore of the Mexican Americans in South Texas. He was professor emeritus of English and anthropology.
<http://clnet.ucr.edu/paredes.html>
<www.dallasnews.com/entertainment/0613books5paredes.htm>

Jack Parsons is a photographer. His photographs illustrate *Low 'N Slow*, a book about low riders in New Mexico.

Teresa Pijoan, Ph.D. is a New Mexico native, storyteller, and author. She has been director of the Native American Story-Theater Troupe and a teacher at Technical Vocational Institute in Albuquerque.
<http://redcrane.com/bilingual/stories.htm>
<www.augusthouse.com/0-87483-155-5.htm>

Jorge Prieto was born in Mexico City. In 1923 his father, a political exile, moved the family to Texas and then to California. Prieto became a doctor and served for more than 35 years in Chicago. He is also the author of *Harvest of Hope*.

Juan Ramirez overcame numerous problems after his experiences in Vietnam. He now owns a landscaping business in California.
<www.unmpress.com/book/0826319599.html>

Kirk Reeve is the author of *Lolo and Red Legs*.
<www.northlandpub.com/store/index.cfm?Render=Browse_Detail&Company=Northland%20Publishing&Book_ID=53&Keywords=>

Samuel O. Regalado, the nephew of a former major league baseball player, is a professor of history at California State University, Stanislaus. His articles on baseball have been published in several periodicals.
<www.csustan.edu/History/Regalado.html>

Luis Reyes is a co-author of *Hispanics in Hollywood*.

David Rice is a native of South Texas. He has written two short story collections and has written and directed plays, films, and a one-man show, "Just a Kid from Edcouch." Rice is writer-in-residence for the Llano Grande Center for Research and Development in Edcouch, Texas.

Alberto Alvaro Ríos, an Arizona native, is the author of several books of poetry and short stories. He is a Regents' Professor at Arizona State University in Tempe.
<http://researchmag.asu.edu/stories/alphabet.html>

Antonio Ríos-Bustamante, Ph.D. is a professor at the University of Arizona, Tucson. He has edited and authored a number of monographs and books, is Coordinator of Historical and Museum Programs, and has produced exhibits and a video documentary.
<http://siswww.uwyo.edu/reg/bulletin/2aschst.html>
<http://w3fp.arizona.edu/masrc/pubs/museo.htm>

Edward Rivera is a writer of Puerto Rican descent.

Oswald Rivera was born in Puerto Rico and now lives in New York. He is the author of a cookbook and a novel about the Vietnam War.

María Robledo Montecel, Ph.D. is executive director of the Intercultural Development Research Association in San Antonio, Texas. She has extensive experience in dropout prevention programs.
<www.idra.org/WhosWho/IDRAStaff.htm#Cuca_Robledo>

Art Rodríguez grew up in San Jose, California. After a troubled youth that included time in a correctional institution, Rodríguez became a successful businessman and is now the author of three books.
<http://pages.prodigy.net/mr_art/meet.html>

Luis J. Rodríguez grew up in Los Angeles, California. A poet, journalist, and critic, Rodríguez founded Tía Chucha Press. He has published poetry, picture books, and a memoir, *Always Running*, and is active in anti-gang activities.
<www.wordsculptors.com/luis/>
<www.lrna.org/league/PT/PT.2001.04/PT.2001.04.9.html>

Richard Rodríguez is a writer and editor. The author of two books, he works as an editor at Pacific News Service in San Francisco, and contributes to *Harper's* and the *Los Angeles Times*. Rodríguez appears on the *MacNeil Lehrer News Hour*.
<www.scottlondon.com/insight/scripts/rodriguez.html>

Robert Rodríguez, one of ten children, developed an interest in movies that began with weekly trips to a San Antonio theater. Rodríguez became a Hollywood director. *El Mariachi* and *Desperado* are two of his works.
<www.exposure.co.uk/makers/minute.html>
<www.godamongdirectors.com/rodriguez/faq/aol.html>

Maritza Romero is the author of several biographies for children.

Regina Romero is a New Mexico native and the author of a cookbook based on her grandmother's recipes. She lives in New Mexico.
<http://weeklywire.com/tw/11-26-98/book3.htm>

Francisco A. Rosales was a high school dropout. He served in the Air Force and later completed his education to become a scholar, historian, and university professor. He lives in Tempe, Arizona.

Joe Rosenberg is a playwright and director. He was born in Poland and learned Spanish after marrying a woman from Mexico. He founded the South Texas Performance Company. A theater scholar, Rosenberg has established bilingual theater programs in several school districts.

Peter Rubic is a co-author of *Hispanics in Hollywood*.

Joseph J. Ruiz is a native of New Mexico. After retirement, Ruiz has been active in community affairs and has published two bilingual children's books.
<www.sunstonepress.com/cgi-bin/bookview.cgi?_recordnum=257>
<www.sunstonepress.com/cgi-bin/bookview.cgi?_recordnum=110>

Mona Ruiz has been a police officer in Santa Ana, California since 1989. Ruiz was a member of a street gang, a young mother, and an abused wife, but she survived and fulfilled her dream of becoming a police officer.

Bryan Ryan is co-editor of two reference books on Hispanics.

Pam Muñoz Ryan grew up in California's San Joaquin Valley. She is the author of several award-winning books for children and young adults. Ryan lives with her family near San Diego, California.
<www.pammunozryan.com/bio.html>

Andrés Sáenz was born in 1927 on the Rancho de Santa Cruz in Duval County, in South Texas. He donated his writings to the University of Texas Institute of Texan Cultures in San Antonio in 1997.
<www.texancultures.utsa.edu/ranching/chapters/toc1.htm>

Floyd Salas is the author of a number of books of fiction as well as autobiographical works.

René Saldaña, Jr. grew up in South Texas. The author of poems, stories, and a novel, he has been an English teacher and is in the doctoral program at Georgia State University.
<www.randomaudiobooks.com/catalog/display.pperl?isbn=0385327250>

Alejo Salinas, Jr., Ph.D. was born in La Reforma, Texas. Salinas has worked in the field of education as a bus driver, a teacher, principal, coordinator of bilingual education, and super-intendent. In addition, he has been a city commissioner and a member of the Board of Trustees of South Texas Community College. He lives in Edinburg, Texas.

Robert Sanabria was born in El Paso, Texas. He is a retired Army Lieutenant Colonel and a veteran of the Korean and Vietnam wars. Sanabria is a sculptor whose works are now in Kentucky, Pennsylvania, Maryland, Virginia, and other locations across the country.
<www.thirdagemedia.com/features/money/work/careers/sanabria.html>

Alex Sanchez is the author of *Rainbow Boys*. He was born in Mexico and has worked as a youth and family counselor for many years.
<www.alexsanchez.com/WhoIsAlex.htm>

Richard Sanchez is the author of a series of nonfiction books on Hispanic heritage.

Esmeralda Santiago is a Puerto Rican author of fiction and nonfiction.
<http://voices.cla.umn.edu/authors/esmeraldasantiago.html>
<www.randomhouse.com/vintage/read/puerto/santiago.html>

John Phillip Santos, the first Mexican-American Rhodes scholar, grew up in San Antonio, Texas. Santos has published numerous newspaper articles and has produced many television documentaries. He works for the Ford Foundation in New York City.
<www.publishersweekly.com/nbf/docs/sethouse_jpsantos.html>
<www.villagevoice.com/issues/9939/morales.php>

Isabel Schon, Ph.D. is Director of the Center for the Study of Books in Spanish for Children and Adolescents at California State University. She is the author of more than twenty reference books and a Spanish-language children's book of rhymes and riddles.
<www.csusm.edu/csb/english/>

Alfonso Silva Lee is a biologist, photographer, and writer. The author of nine books and numerous articles, he lives in the mountains of Puerto Rico.
<www.pangaea.org/authors_pangaea/silva.htm>

Gary Soto is the author of novels, short stories, drama, poetry, and biography for children and adults. The recipient of numerous awards, Soto lives and works in California.
<http://falcon.jmu.edu/~ramseyil/soto.htm>

Virgil Suárez was born in Cuba in 1962. The author of several novels and short stories, he also has worked as an editor for several anthologies. Suárez teaches creative writing at Florida State University. He lives with his wife and two daughters in Tallahassee.
<http://english.fsu.edu/faculty/vsuarez.htm>
<www.wingspress.com/vsuarez.html>

Charles Sullivan has been a teacher, has served in government and public service positions, and is currently Dean of the Graduate School of Arts and Sciences at Georgetown University. He is responsible for several award-winning books that combine literature and art.

Phyllis Tashlik is a public school teacher in New York City. She works with teen writers at the Urban Academy, an alternative high school.

Piri Thomas, author of *Down These Mean Streets*, was born in 1928 in New York City. After a troubled youth and years in prison, Thomas worked with street gangs in Spanish Harlem and in Puerto Rico in the field of rehabilitation of drug addiction.
<www.cheverote.com/bio.html>
<www.inmotionmagazine.com/thomas.html>
<www.speakersandartists.org/People/PiriThomas.html>

Andrés Tijerina, Ph.D. is a professor of history at Austin Community College. Tijerina has authored several books about Tejano history.
<www2.austin.cc.tx.us/tijnotes.VITA.html>

Reies López Tijerina was a key figure in the New Mexico land grant protests of 1960s.
<http://weeklywire.com/ww/06-13-97/alibi_feat1.html>
<www.aztlan.net/treatynm.htm>

Eric Tomb has produced books for Bellerophon Books in California.

John A. (Albert) Torres is the author of several sports biographies and is a newspaper reporter for the *Poughkeepsie Journal* in New York. He and his family live in Fishkill, New York where he enjoys fishing and coaching Little League baseball.

Charley Trujillo is a native of Corcoran, California. He served in Vietnam and earned a Purple Heart and a Bronze Star. Trujillo received degrees from the University of California, Berkeley and San Jose State University. He is an instructor of intercultural studies at De Anza College in Cupertino, California.
<www.agif.org/soldados.html>

Frances Esquibel Tywoniak was born in New Mexico and grew up in California in a farm worker family. She was one of the first Mexican Americans to attend the University of California, Berkeley. Tywoniak is a retired teacher and administrator.
<www.ucpress.edu/books/pages/8476.html>

Sabine R. Ulibarrí was born in New Mexico in 1919. A veteran of World War II, he has written short stories, Spanish-language textbooks, and a memoir. He received a New Mexico Governor's Award and a Pioneer Award from the National Association for Bilingual Education. He served as a professor at the University of New Mexico and is recognized as a civic leader.
<www.tqsbooks.com/HISTORY_PICS/Sabine_Ulibarri.html>

Luis Alberto Urrea is an award-winning novelist, essayist, poet, and teacher. He lives with his wife and family in Lafayette, Louisiana where he is Writer in Residence at the University of Southwestern Louisiana.
<www.luisurrea.com/works/works.htm>
<www.uapress.arizona.edu/books/BID1226.htm>
<www.cincopuntos.com/ghostsic.html>

Carmen Aboy Valldejuli, a Puerto Rican author of cookbooks and a children's book, works with her husband on recipes.
<http://pelicanpub.com/cookbooks/juntos-en-la-cocina.htm>

Mary Lau Valle is the co-author of a cookbook. She has taught at California Polytech State University at San Luis Obispo.
<www.thenewpress.com/books/recipe.htm>

Victor M. Valle teaches journalism and writes for the *Los Angeles Times*.
<www.thenewpress.com/books/recipe.htm>

Gloria Velásquez is the author of five books for teens and a book and sound recording of poetry. She is a teacher at California Polytechnic State University in San Luis Obispo.
<http://cla.calpoly.edu/~gvelasqu/main.html>

Angel Vigil has written books on folklore and drama. He is chairman of the Fine and Performing Arts Department of Colorado Academy in Denver. Vigil is also a stage director, performer, and storyteller.
<www.fulcrum-resources.com/html/vigil.html>

Victor Villaseñor grew up on a ranch near San Diego, California. Despite his dyslexia, he became a successful author of several award-winning biographies, a novel, and screenplays.

Lea Ybarra is a teacher, researcher, and community activist. She is executive director of the Academic Advancement of Youth at Johns Hopkins University in Maryland.
<www.twbookmark.com/authors/7/1591/index.html>

Chapter 10

Other Latino Writers

The following is a list of Latino authors who were not otherwise included in this guide. Some of the writers listed in this section have not written books that are specifically for children or young adults. Others have written books that are included in *Picture Books by Latino Writers* (Linworth Publishing, Inc. 2002). Yet others may be the authors of books that for some reason did not fit the criteria for inclusion in this guide or the picture books guide.

Some works by these authors are long out of print but are included for those wishing to pursue historical aspects of Latino literature. Some of these Latino writers have works in progress or in mind for the future that will be suitable for younger readers. Others may have gained notice by winning awards or by having their works published in anthologies.

This list is offered for readers seeking additional Latino-authored books for their own purposes. It is not all-inclusive and should be considered a starting point. Any omissions are inadvertent. With so many talented Latino writers being recognized across the country, this list should grow longer with the passage of time.

CA = Cuban American
DA = Dominican American
MA = Mexican American
PR = Puerto Rican

A

Alex Abella (CA) *Fiction*

Oscar "Zeta" Acosta (MA) *Fiction*

Teresa Palomo Acosta (MA) *Nonfiction*

Rodolfo Acuña (MA) *Nonfiction*

Jack Agüeros (PR) *Short Stories, Poetry*

Jorge H. Aigla (MA) *Poetry*

Francisco X. Alarcón (MA) *Poetry*

Kathleen Alcalá (MA) *Fiction*

Arturo Aldama (MA) *Nonfiction*

Miguel Algarín (PR) *Poetry*

Isabel Allende (Chilean) Fiction, *Nonfiction*

Félix D. Almaráz (MA) *Nonfiction*

Alurista (MA) *Poetry*

Julia Alvarez (DA) *Fiction, Poetry*

Alba Ambert (PR) *Poetry, Nonfiction*

Luis Alberto Ambroggio (Argentina) *Poetry*

Gloria Anzaldúa (MA) *Nonfiction*

Daniel Aragón y Ulibarrí (MA) *Fiction*

Juan Estevan Arellano (MA) *Fiction, Nonfiction*

Reinaldo Arenas (CA) *Fiction*

Ron Arias (MA) *Fiction*

Alfred Arteaga (MA) *Poetry, Nonfiction*

Elena Avila (MA) Drama, Poetry, Nonfiction

Vernon Avila (PR) *Fiction*

Naomi Ayala (PR) *Poetry*

B

Ana Baca (MA) *Fiction*

Jimmy Santiago Baca (MA) *Poetry, Nonfiction*

Joan Baez (MA) *Nonfiction*

Francisco E. Balderrama (MA) *Nonfiction*

Octavio A. Ballesteros (MA) *Nonfiction*

Aida Barrera (MA) *Nonfiction*

Sandra Benítez (PR) *Fiction*

Charles Ramírez Berg (MA) *Nonfiction*

Richard Bertematti (CA) *Fiction*

James Carlos Blake (MA) Fiction, *Short Stories*

María del Carmen Boza (CA) *Nonfiction*

Manuel B. Bravo (MA) *Nonfiction*

Aristeo Brito (MA) *Fiction*

Bruce-Novoa (MA) *Nonfiction*

José Antonio Burciaga (MA) *Poetry*

Julia de Burgos (PR) *Poetry*

C

Guillermo Cabrera Infante (CA) *Fiction*

Nash Candelaria (MA) *Fiction*

Daniel Cano (MA) *Fiction*

Norma Elia Cantú (MA) *Fiction*

Alvaro Cardona-Hine (Costa Rica) *Poetry*

Mariah Carey *Nonfiction*

Louis Carrillo *Nonfiction*

Carlos Eduardo Castañeda (MA) *Nonfiction*

Olivia Castellano (MA) *Fiction, Poetry*

Ana Castillo (MA) *Fiction, Poetry*

Rosemary Catacalos (MA) *Poetry*

Orlando Cepeda (PR) *Nonfiction*

Lorna Dee Cervantes (MA) *Poetry*

Ernesto E. Cervantez (MA) *Nonfiction*

Daniel Chacón (MA) *Short Stories*

Rafael Chacón (MA) *Nonfiction*

Veronica Chambers (Panamanian) *Nonfiction*

Becky Chavarría-Cháirez (MA) *Fiction*

Denise Chávez (MA) *Fiction, Drama*

Jaime Chávez (MA) *Poetry*

Linda Chávez (MA) *Nonfiction*
María Chaviel (MA) *Fiction*
Ralph Cintron (MA) *Nonfiction*
Sandra Cisneros (MA) *Fiction, Short Stories, Poetry*
Jesús Colón (PR) *Nonfiction*
Juan Contreras (MA) *Poetry, Nonfiction*
Arsenio Córdova (MA) *Nonfiction*
Lucha Corpi (MA) *Fiction*
Jesús C. Corral (MA) *Nonfiction*
Rodolfo J. Cortina (CA) *Drama*
Angie Cruz (DA) *Fiction*
Bill Cruz *Nonfiction*
Victor Hernández Cruz (PR) *Poetry*
Carlos Cumpián (MA) *Poetry*

D

Angela De Hoyos (MA) *Poetry*
Greta de León Anchondo (MA) *Poetry*
María Isabel Delgado (MA) *Poetry*
Elena Díaz (MA) *Fiction*
Emilio Díaz (Puerto Rico) *Fiction*
Junot Díaz (DA) *Fiction*
Tony Diaz (MA) *Fiction*
Arthur Dorros (MA) *Fiction*
Stella Pope Duarte (MA) *Short Stories*
Roberto Durán (MA) *Poetry*

E

Sergio Elizondo (MA) *Poetry*
Virgilio P. Elizondo (MA) *Nonfiction*
Margarita Engle (CA) *Fiction*
María Amparo Escandón (MA) *Fiction*
Martín Espada (PR) *Fiction, Poetry*
Laura Esquivel (Mexican) *Fiction*
Sandra María Esteves (PR) *Poetry*

F

Roberto G. Fernández (CA) *Fiction*
Rosario Ferré (PR) *Fiction*
Figueredo, D. H.

G

Mary Sue Galindo (MA) *Fiction, Poety*
Sallie Gallegos (MA) *Fiction*
Cristina García (CA) *Fiction*
Diana García (MA) *Poetry*
Eric García *Fiction*
Guy García (MA) *Fiction*
María García (MA) *Fiction*
Mario T. García (MA) *Nonfiction*
Nasario García (MA) *Nonfiction*
Pelayo "Pete" García (CA) *Fiction*
Ricardo L. García (MA) *Fiction, Poetry*
Carolina García-Aguilera (CA) *Fiction*
Cecilio García Camarillo (MA) *Poetry*
Victoria García-Zapata (MA) *Poetry*

Leticia M. Garza-Falcón (MA) *Nonfiction*

Frank X. Gaspar (Portuguese) *Fiction, Poetry*

Alicia Gaspar de Alba (MA) *Fiction, Short Stories, Poetry, Nonfiction*

Dagoberto Gilb (MA) *Fiction, Short Stories*

Fabiola Cabeza de Baca Gilbert (MA) *Nonfiction*

Guillermo Gómez-Peña (MA) *Poetry*

Edward Gonzales (MA) *Nonfiction*

Gloria Gonzales *Poetry*

Genaro González (MA) *Fiction, Short Stories*

Jovita González Mireles (MA) *Fiction*

Juan González (PR) *Nonfiction*

Louie The Foot González (MA) *Nonfiction*

Ray González (MA) *Poetry*

Rigoberto González (MA) *Poetry*

Rosie González (MA) *Nonfiction*

Luis F. González-Cruz (CA) *Drama*

Mari Graña (MA) *Nonfiction*

Alejandro Grattan-Domínguez (MA) *Fiction*

Evelio Grillo (CA) *Nonfiction*

Lucrecia Guerrero (MA) *Short Stories*

Jorge Guitart (CA) *Nonfiction*

Celeste Guzmán (MA) *Poetry*

H

Armand Hernández (MA) *Poetry*

Inés Hernández (MA) *Poetry*

Andrea O'Reilly Herrera (CA) *Fiction*

Juan Felipe Herrera (MA) *Poetry, Nonfiction*

Juanita Herrera *Nonfiction*

María Herrera-Sobek (MA) *Nonfiction*

Oscar Hijuelos (CA) *Fiction*

María Hinojosa (MA) *Nonfiction*

Rolando Hinojosa (MA) *Fiction*

Tish Hinojosa (MA) *Nonfiction*

Carolina Hospital (CA) *Fiction*

Jorge Huerta (MA) *Drama*

I

Arturo Islas (MA) *Fiction*

J

Cleofas M. Jaramillo (MA) *Nonfiction*

Carlos M. Jiménez (MA) *Nonfiction*

Randall C. Jiménez (MA) *Poetry*

Miguel Juárez (MA) *Nonfiction*

K

Nicolás Kanellos (PR) *Drama*

Gary Keller (MA) Fiction, *Short Stories*

Elisa Kleven *Fiction*

Edward García Kraul (MA) *Nonfiction*

L

Tato Laviera (PR) *Poetry*

Luís Leal (MA) *Nonfiction*

John Leguizamo (PR) *Drama*

Aurora Levins Morales (PR) *Fiction, Short Stories*

María Leyba (MA) *Fiction, Short Stories, Poetry, Nonfiction*
Graciela Limón (MA) *Fiction*
Arturo Longoria (MA) *Nonfiction*
Jack López (MA) *Short Stories*
Josefina López (MA) *Drama*
Loretta López (MA) *Fiction*
Nancy López (MA) *Nonfiction*
Consuelo Luz (MA) *Poetry*

M

Eduardo Machado (CA) *Drama*
Amalio Madueño (MA) *Poetry*
Carl Marcum (MA) *Poetry*
E. A. Mares (MA) *Poetry*
Cheech Marin (MA) *Fiction*
José Martí (CA) *Poetry*
Patricia Preciado Martin (MA) *Short Stories*
Al Martínez (MA) *Fiction*
Demetria Martínez (MA) *Poetry*
Manuel Luis Martínez (MA) *Fiction*
Matt Martínez (MA) *Nonfiction*
Max Martínez (MA) *Fiction*
Rubén Martínez (MA) *Nonfiction*
Valerie Martínez (MA) *Poetry*
Zarela Martínez (MA) *Nonfiction*
Hugo Martínez-Serros (MA) *Short Stories*
Julio Marzán (PR) *Poetry, Short Stories*
Oliver Mayer (MA) *Drama*
Wendell Mayo (MA) *Fiction, Short Stories*
Jacqueline Higuera McMahan (MA) *Nonfiction*
CC. Medina (CA) *Fiction*
Pablo Medina (CA) *Poetry, Short Stories*

Ana Méndez (CA) *Short Stories*
Miguel Méndez M. (MA) *Nonfiction*
Nancy Mercado (PR) *Poetry*
Jerry Mondragon (MA) *Drama, Poetry*
David Nava Monreal (MA) *Short Stories, Drama*
Carolina Monsivaís (MA) *Poetry*
Mary Montaño (MA) *Nonfiction*
José Montoya (MA) *Nonfiction*
Richard Montoya (MA) *Drama*
Joshua Al Mora (MA) *Drama*
Cherríe Moraga (MA) *Drama, Poetry, Nonfiction*
Alejandro Morales (MA) *Fiction*
Rodney Morales (PR) *Short Stories*
Raul Morin (MA) *Nonfiction*
Carlos Muñoz, Jr. (MA) *Nonfiction*
Elías Miguel Muñoz (CA) *Fiction*
Yxta Maya Murray (MA) *Fiction*

N

Rick Najera (MA) *Drama*
Michael Nava (MA) *Fiction*
Laura Navarro (MA) *Nonfiction*
S. D. Navarro (MA) *Short Stories*
Elizabeth Loza Newby (MA) *Nonfiction*
Josefina Niggli (MA) *Fiction, Drama*
Carmen Santiago Nodar (PR) *Fiction*
Chon A. Noriega (MA) *Nonfiction*
Himilce Novas (CA) *Fiction*

O

Achy Obejas (CA) *Fiction, Short Stories*
Cynthia Orozco (MA) *Nonfiction*
Cristina Ortega (MA) *Fiction*

P

Ana Pacheco *Nonfiction*
Genaro M. Padilla (MA) *Nonfiction*
Heberto Padilla (CA) *Fiction*
Américo Paredes (MA) *Fiction, Short Stories*
Amado M. Peña, Jr. (MA) *Nonfiction*
Terri de la Peña (MA) *Fiction*
Willie Perdomo (PR) *Poetry*
Amada Irma Pérez (MA) *Fiction*
Frank Pérez *Nonfiction*
Loida Maritza Pérez (DA) *Fiction*
Luis Pérez (MA) *Fiction, Nonfiction*
Gustavo Pérez Firmat (CA) *Fiction, Poetry*
Pedro Pietri (PR) *Poetry*
Ricardo Pimentel (MA) *Fiction*
Cecile Pineda *Fiction*
Miguel Piñero (PR) *Drama, Poetry*
Nicole Pollentier (MA) *Poetry*
Mary Helen Ponce (MA) *Fiction, Nonfiction*
Estela Portillo Trambley (MA) *Fiction, Short Stories, Drama*
Dolores Prida (CA) *Drama*
Raquel Puig Zaldivar (CA) *Fiction*

Q

J. Gilberto Quezada (MA) *Nonfiction*
Ernesto Peña Quiñonez (PR) *Fiction*
Leroy V. Quintana (MA) *Poetry*
Jacinto Quirarte (MA) *Nonfiction*

R

Manuel Ramos (MA) Fiction
Raúlrsalinas (MA) *Poetry*
Tey Diana Rebolledo (MA) *Nonfiction*
John Rechy (MA) *Fiction*
David Reyes (MA) *Nonfiction*
Thelma Reyna (MA) *Short Stories, Poetry*
Feliciano Ribera (MA) *Nonfiction*
Alberto Alvaro Ríos (MA) *Short Stories, Poetry, Nonfiction*
José Rivera (PR) *Drama*
Rick Rivera (MA) *Fiction*
Rowena A. Rivera (MA) *Nonfiction*
Tomás Rivera (MA) *Short Stories*
Louie García Robinson (MA) *Fiction*
Rodolfo Rocha (MA) *Nonfiction*
Abraham Rodríguez (PR) *Fiction, Short Stories*
Aleida Rodríguez (CA) *Poetry*
Andrés Rodríguez (MA) *Poetry*
Janel Rodríguez *Nonfiction*
Jeanette Rodríguez (MA) *Nonfiction*
Mary Grace Rodríguez (MA) *Poetry*
Raymond Rodríguez (MA) *Nonfiction*
Octavio I. Romano-V (MA) *Nonfiction*
Danny Romero (MA) *Fiction*
Leo Romero (MA) *Short Stories, Poetry*
Levi Romero (MA) *Poetry*

Abel G. Rubio (MA) *Nonfiction*
Francisco Ruiz *Fiction*
Ronald L. Ruiz (MA) *Fiction*
Vicki L. Ruiz (MA) *Nonfiction*

S

Benjamin Alire Sáenz (MA) Fiction
José David Saldívar (MA) *Nonfiction*
Ramón Saldívar (MA) *Nonfiction*
Luis Omar Salinas (MA) *Poetry*
Marta Salinas (MA) *Short Stories*
George I. Sánchez (MA) *Nonfiction*
Irene Sánchez (MA) *Nonfiction*
Joseph P. Sánchez (MA) *Nonfiction*
Ricardo Sánchez (MA) *Poetry*
Rosaura Sánchez (MA) *Nonfiction*
Carlos Santana (MA) *Nonfiction*
Loreina Santos Silva (PR) *Poetry, Nonfiction*
Yvonne V. Sapia (PR) *Fiction, Poetry*
Alberto Sarraín (CA) *Drama*
José Sequeira (Nicaraguan) *Short Stories, Poetry*
Michele Serros (MA) *Fiction*
Herbert Siguenza (MA) *Drama*
Beverly Silva (MA) *Short Stories, Poetry*
Simón Silva (MA) *Nonfiction*
José Skinner (MA) *Fiction, Short Stories*
Martin Cruz Smith (MA) *Fiction*
Joseph Somoza (MA) *Poetry*
Lionel Sosa (MA) *Nonfiction*
Pedro Juan Soto (PR) *Fiction, Short Stories*
Ilan Stavans (MA) *Nonfiction*
Jan Romero Stevens (MA) *Fiction, Nonfiction*
Francisco X. Stork (MA) *Fiction*

Virgil Suárez (CA) *Fiction, Short Stories, Poetry*
Maite Suárez-Rivas (MA) *Nonfiction*

T

Carmen Tafolla (MA) *Poetry*
Sheila Ortiz Taylor (MA) *Fiction*
Jesús F. de la Teja *Nonfiction*
Raymond L. Telles (MA) *Nonfiction*

Jane Tenorio-Coscarelli (MA) *Fiction, Nonfiction*
Aimée Thurlo (CA) *Fiction*
Larry Torres (MA) *Drama*
Olga Beatriz Torres (Mexican) *Nonfiction*
Edwin Torres (PR) *Fiction*
Leyla Torres (MA) *Fiction*
Frances Marie Treviño (MA) *Poetry*
Jesús Salvador Treviño (MA) *Short Stories*
Lee Treviño (MA) *Nonfiction*
Sergio Troncoso (MA) *Short Stories*
Charley Trujillo (MA) *Fiction*

U

Sabine R. Ulibarrí (MA) *Short Stories*
Luis Alberto Urrea (MA) *Fiction*

V

Gina Valdés (MA) *Poetry*
Luis Valdez (MA) *Drama*
Leonard A. Valverde (MA) *Nonfiction*
Gloria Vando (PR) *Poetry*
Diego Vázquez, Jr. (MA) *Fiction*
Sarah Vázquez Fiction, *Nonfiction*
Alfredo Véa (MA) *Fiction*
Ana Veciana-Suárez (CA) *Fiction*
Denise Vega (MA) *Fiction*
Ed Vega (PR) *Fiction, Short Stories*
Evangelina Vigil-Piñón (MA) *Poetry*
Alma Luz Villanueva (MA) *Poetry*
Tino Villanueva (MA) *Poetry*
José Antonio Villarreal (MA) *Fiction*
Rosa Martha Villarreal (MA) *Fiction*
Marcos McPeek Villatoro (MA) *Fiction*
Leonor Villegas de Magnón (MA) *Nonfiction*
Helena María Viramontes (MA) *Fiction, Short*
    Stories

Y

José Yglesias (CA) *Fiction*
Jonathan Yorba (Latino/Pacific Islander)
    Nonfiction
Rosa Elena Yzquierdo (MA) *Short Stories,*
    Poetry

Z

Bernice Zamora (MA) *Poetry*
Emilio Zamora (MA) *Nonfiction*

Nearly Latinos

In the process of researching for this guide, several writers and storytellers who might be categorized as "nearly Latinos" were encountered.

Carrie Sue Ayvar is a bilingual storyteller and teacher from Florida. Ayvar is dedicated to promoting storytelling in the United States and Mexico. Her bilingual storytelling audiotape is *Cuentame un Cuento/Tell Me a Story*. She is originally from Pennsylvania, is of Eastern European descent, and her husband is originally from Mexico.

Deborah Blanche considers herself born to be a storyteller. She is a Spanish speaker but is not Latina. Blanche actively pursues her calling as a bilingual storyteller.

Joe Hayes is a bilingual storyteller and is the author of a number of bilingual books. A native of Arizona, Hayes is an active storyteller, often appearing at library and reading conferences. He is the resident storyteller at the Wheelwright Museum of the American Indian in Santa Fe, New Mexico.

Lea Hernandez' *Cathedral Child* was nominated for the ALA Popular Paperbacks for Young Adults in the graphic novels category. Her other graphic novel is *Clockwork Angels*. Hernandez, Latina by marriage, is also a co-author of *Elfquest—New Blood*.

Bryce Milligan has experience as a book critic, folksinger, college teacher, journalist, editor, poet, playwright, and director of the literature program at the Guadalupe Cultural Arts Center in San Antonio, Texas. With Sandra Cisneros he co-founded the Annual Texas Small Press Bookfair, which has evolved into the San Antonio Inter-American Bookfair. The editor/publisher of Wings Press, Milligan has edited several anthologies, including *Daughters of the Fifth Sun*, and teaches creative writing at a high school in San Antonio. <www.wingspress.com>

Amado Muro was a pseudonym for Charles Seltzer, author of *Collected Stories of Amado Muro* published in 1971. Seltzer took his pen name from the maiden name of his Mexican wife, Amada Muro.

Jim Sagel wrote a number of award-winning bilingual books during his lifetime. Among Sagel's books are *Always the Heart/Siempre el Corazón*, a love story for adolescents, *Where the Cinnamon Winds Blow/Donde soplan los vientos de canela*, a novel for younger readers, and *Garden of Stories/Jardín de cuentos*, folklore for young adults. His literature was awarded prizes in Cuba, in Spain, and in the United States.

Danny Santiago is the pen name of Daniel James, author of *Famous All Over Town*.

Michelle L. Trujillo is Latina by marriage and family culture. Her book, *Why Can't We Talk? What Teens Would Share If Parents Would Listen: A Book for Teens* is supported by a Web site <www.whycantwetalk.com>. A former teacher, she lives with her family in Nevada.

Publishers

A. Salinas, Dr. Alejo Salinas, Jr., Hidalgo I.S.D., PO Drawer D, Hidalgo, Texas 78557

ABC-CLIO, 130 Cremona Drive, Santa Barbara, CA 93117, Telephone: 800-368-6868, Fax: 805-685-9685, Web site: <http://abc-clio.com>

Abdo & Daughters, 4940 Viking Drive, Suite 622, Edina, MN 55435, Telephone: 800-800-1312, Fax: 952-831-1632, Web site: <www.abdopub.com>

Arte Público Press, University of Houston, Houston, TX 77204-2174, Telephone: 713-743-2846, Fax: 713-743-3080, Web site: <www.arte-uh.edu>

Bellerophon Books, PO Box 21307, Santa Barbara, CA 93121, Telephone: 800-253-9943, Fax: 805-965-8286, Web site: <www.bellerophonbooks.com>

Bilingual Press/Editorial Bilingüe, Arizona State University, PO Box 872702, Tempe, AZ 85287-2702, Telephone: 480-965-3867, Fax: 480-965-8309, Web site: <www.asu.edu/brp>

Capital Books, International Publishers Marketing, Inc., PO Box 605, Herndon, VA 20172-0605, Telephone: 703-661-1586, 800-758-3756, Fax: 703-661-1501

Chelsea House, 65250 Baltimore Pike, Yeadon, PA 19050, Telephone: 800-362-9786, Fax: 610-359-1439, Web site: <www.chelseahouse.com>

Children's Book Press, 2211 Mission Street, San Francisco, CA 94110, Telephone: 415-821-3080, Fax: 415-821-3081, Web site: <www.cbookpress.org>

Cinco Puntos Press, 701 Texas, El Paso, Texas 79930, Telephone: 800-566-9072, Web site: <www.cincopuntos.com>

Curbstone Press, 321 Jackson Street, Willimantic, CT 06226-1738, Telephone: 860-423-5110, Fax: 860-423-9242, Web site: <www.curbstone.org>

Dream House Press, 2714 Ophelia Ct., San Jose, CA 95122, Telephone: 480-274-4574, Fax: 408-274-0786, Web site: <www.EastSideDreams.com>

Eakin Press, P.O Box 90159, Austin, TX 78709-0159, Telephone: 512-288-1771, Fax: 512-288-1813, Web site: <www.eakinpress.com>

El Centro de la Raza, 2524 16th Avenue South, Seattle, WA 98144

Enslow, Box 398, 40 Industrial Rd., Berkeley Heights, NJ 07922-0398, Telephone: 908-771-9400, Fax: 908-771-0925, Web site: <www.enslow.com>

Exit Studio, 1466 N. Quinn St., Arlington, VA 22209, Telephone: 703-312-7121, Fax: 703-312-6217, Web site: <www.exitstudio.com>

Facts on File, 132 W. 31st Street, 17th Floor, New York, NY 10001, Telephone: 800-322-8755, Fax: 800-678-3633, Web site: <www.factsonfile.com>

Four Walls Eight Windows, 39 West 14th Street, No. 503, New York, NY 10011, Telephone: 800-788-3123, 212-206-8965, Fax: 212-206-8799, Web site: <www.fourwallseightwindows.com/>

Fulcrum Publishing, 16100 Table Mountain Parkway, Suite 300, Golden, CO 80403-1672, Telephone: 800-992-2908, 303-277-1623, Fax: 800-726-7112, 303-279-7111, Web site: <www.fulcrum-books.com>

Harcourt Children's Books, 525 B Street, Suite 1900, San Diego, CA 92101, Telephone: 619-699-6301, Fax: 619-699-6777, Web site: <www.harcourt.com>

HarperCollins, 10 East 53rd Street, New York, NY 10022, Telephone: 212-207-7000, Web site: <www.harpercollins.com>

Henry Holt and Company, 115 West 18th Street, New York, NY 10011, Telephone: 212-886-9200, Fax: 212-645-5832

Historical Science Publishing, Box 2284, Saratoga, CA 95070-0284,
Telephone: 408-727-3640, Fax: 408-727-4577, Web site: <www.hsp-aztec.com>

Intercultural Development Research Association, 5835 Callaghan Road, Suite 350,
San Antonio, TX 78228-1190, Telephone: 210-444-1710, Fax: 210-444-1714, Web site:
<www.idra.org>

John Wiley & Sons, One Wiley Drive, Somerset, NJ 08875, Fax: 732-302-2300

Krieger Publishing, PO Box 9542, Melbourne, FL 32902, Telephone: 321-724-9542,
Fax: 321-951-3671

Lerner Publishing, 241 First Avenue North, Minneapolis, MN 55401-1607,
Telephone: 612-332-3344, 800-328-4929, Fax: 612-332-7615,
Web site: <www.lernerbooks.com>

Libraries Unlimited and Teacher Ideas Press, PO Box 6633, Englewood, CO 80155-6633,
Telephone: 303-770-1220, 800-237-6124, Fax: 303-220-8843, Web site: <www.lu.com>

Little, Brown, and Company, 1271 Avenue of the Americas, New York, NY 10020

Los Abuelos Press, PO Box 9301, Palm Springs, CA 92240

Los Andes, PO Box 190, Chino Hills, CA 91709, Telephone: 626-810-6180,
Fax: 626-810-0419, Web site: <www.LosAndes.com>

Millbrook Press, PO Box 18001, Bridgeport, CT 06601-2801, Telephone: 203-740-2220,
Web site: <www.millbrookpress.com>

Mitchell Lane Publishers, 34 Decidedly Lane, Bear, DE 19701, Telephone: 302-834-9646,
Fax: 302-834-4164, Web site: <www.angelfire.com/biz/mitchelllane.index.html>

Museum of New Mexico Press, PO Box 2087, Santa Fe, NM 87504

The New Press, 450 W. 41st St., New York, NY 10036, Telephone: 212-629-8811,
Fax: 212-629-8617, Web site: <www.thenewpress.com/>

Northland Publishing/Rising Moon, PO Box 1389, Flagstaff, AZ 86002-1389, Telephone: 800-346-3257 (U.S.), 520-774-5251 (outside U.S.), Web site: <www.northlandpub.com>

Pangaea, 226 Wheeler Street South, Saint Paul, MN 55105-1927, Telephone: 651-690-3320, Fax: 651-690-1485, Web site: <www.pangaea.org>

Peachtree Publishers, 1700 Chattahoochee Avenue, Atlanta, GA 30318-2112, Telephone: 404-876-8791, 800-241-0113, Fax: 404-875-2578, 800-875-8909, Web site: <www.peachtree-online.com>

Pelican Publishing, PO Box 3110, Gretna, LA 70054-3110, Telephone: 504-368-1175, Fax: 504-368-1195, Web site: <www.pelicanpub.com>

Penguin Putnam, Academic Marketing Dept., 375 Hudson Street, New York, NY 10014-3657, Telephone: 212-366-2372, Web site: <www.penguinputnam.com>

Persea Books, 60 Madison Avenue, New York, NY 10010, Telephone: 212-779-7668, Fax: 212-689-5405

Peter Smith Publisher, 5 Lexington Avenue, Magnolia, MA 01930-3998

Players Press, PO Box 1132, 4624 Fulton Ave., Unit 31, Studio City, CA 91614-0132

Plume, 375 Hudson Street, New York, NY 10014, Telephone: 212-366-2222, Fax: 212-366-2262

powerHouse Books, 180 Varick Street, Suite 1302, New York, NY 10014, Telephone: 212-604-9074, Fax: 212-366-5247, Web site: <www.powerHouseBooks.com>

Raintree Steck-Vaughn, 15 East 26th Street, New York, NY 10010, Telephone: 646-935-3702, Fax: 646-935-3713, Web site: <www.steckvaughn.com>

Random House Children's Books, 1540 Broadway, New York, NY, Web site: <www.randomhouse.com>

Red Crane Books, PO Box 33950, Santa Fe, NM 87594, Telephone: 505-988-7070, Fax: 505-989-7476, Web site: <www.redcrane.com>

Renaissance Learning, Accelerated Reader, PO Box 8036, Wisconsin Rapids, WI 54495-8036, Telephone: 800-338-4204, 715-424-3636, Fax: 715-424-4242, Web site: <www.renlearn.com/>

Rosen Publishing, 25 West 26th Street, New York, NY 10010, Telephone: 212-777-3017, Fax: 212-684-9127, Web site: <www.rosenpublishing.com>

Royal Fireworks Press, First Avenue, PO Box 399, Unionville, NY 10988-0399, Telephone: 914-726-4444, Fax: 914-726-3824

S. Martinez, Soraida Martinez, 10 Foster Ave., C-1, Gibbsboro, NJ 08026, Telephone: 856-346-3131, Fax: 856-346-3251, Web site: <www.soraida.com>

Scholastic, 557 Broadway, New York, NY 10012 Telephone: 212-343-6100, Web site: <www.scholastic.com> Reading Counts Telephone: 877-268-6871, Web site: <http:src.scholastic.com/ecatalog/>

Seal Press, 3131 Western Avenue, Suite 410, Seattle, WA 98121, Web site: 206-283-7844, 800-788-3123 (orders), Fax: 206-285-9410, Web site: <www.sealpress.com>

Seven Stories Press, 140 Watts Street, New York, NY 10013, Telephone: 212-226-1411, Web site: <www.sevenstories.com>

Silver Moon Press, 160 Fifth Avenue, New York, NY 10010, Telephone: 212-242-6499, 800-874-3320, Fax: 212-242-6799, Web site: <www.silvermoonpress.com/>

Simon & Schuster, 1230 Avenue of Americas, New York, NY 10020, Telephone: 800-223-2336, Fax: 212-698-4350

South End Press, 7 Brookline St. #1, Cambridge, MA 02139-4146, Telephone: 617-547-4002, Fax: 617-547-1333, Web site: <www.southendpress.org>

Sunstone Press, Box 2321, Santa Fe, NM 87504-2321, Telephone: 800-243-5644, Fax: 505-988-1025, Web site: <www.sunstonepress.com>

Texas A&M University Press, Lewis St., Lindsey Bldg., 4354 TAMU, College Station, TX 77843-4354, Telephone: 979-845-1436, 800-826-8911, Fax: 888-617-2421, Web site: <www.tamu.edu/upress/>

Texas Tech University Press, Box 41037, Lubbock, TX 79409-1037, Telephone: 800-832-4042, Web site: <www.ttup.ttu.edu>

Thwack! Pow! Productions, PO Box 751060, Petaluma, CA 94975-1060, Telephone: 707-793-0248, Fax: 707-792-2944, Web site: <www.sonic.net> <www.sonic.net/~comix/comp_t.shtml#Thwack!_Pow!_Productions>

Time Warner Trade Publishing, 332 South Enterprise Boulevard, Lebanon, IN 46052, Telephone: 800-759-0190, Fax: 800-331-1664

TQS Publications, PO Box 9275, Berkeley, CA 94709, Telephone: 510-655-8036, Fax: 510-601-6938, Web site: <www.tqsbooks.com>

Treasure Chest Books/Rio Nuevo Publishers, PO Box 5250, Tucson, AZ 85703, Telephone: 520-623-9558, Fax: 520-624-5888, Web site: <www.rionuevo.com>

University of Arizona Press, 355 S. Euclid Avenue, Suite 103, Tucson , AZ 85719-6654, Telephone: 520-621-1441, Fax: 520-621-8899, Web site: <www.uapress.arizona.edu>

University of California Press, 1095 Essex Street, Richmond, CA 94801, Telephone: 609-883-1759, Fax: 609-883-7413, Web site: <www.ucpress.edu>

University of Chicago Press, 1427 East 60th Street, Chicago, IL 60637, Telephone: 773-702-7700, Fax: 773-702-9756, Web site: <www.press.uchicago.edu>

University of Illinois Press, 1325 South Oak Street, Champaign, IL 61820, Fax: 217-244-8082, Web site: <www.uillinois.edu>

University of Minnesota Press, 111 Third Avenue South, Suite 290, Minneapolis, MN 55401-2520, Telephone: 612-627-1970, Fax: 612-627-1980, Web site: <www.upress.umn.edu/>

University of New Mexico Press, 1720 Lomas Blvd. NE, Albuquerque, NM 87131-1591, Telephone: 505-277-7553, Fax: 505-277-9270, Web site: <www.unmpress.com>

University Press of Colorado, 5589 Arapahoe Road, Suite 206C, Boulder, CO 80303, Telephone: 720-406-8849, Fax: 720-406-3443

U X L Gale Group, PO Box 9187, Farmington Hills, MI 48333-9187, Telephone: 800-877-4253, Fax: 800-414-5043, Web site: <www.galegroup.com>

VGM Career Horizons, 4255 Touhy Avenue, Lincolnwood, Illinois 60712-1975

Warner Bros. Publications, 15800 N.W. 48th Avenue, Miami, FL 33014, Fax: 305-621-4869

Wings Press, 627 E. Guenther, San Antonio, TX 78210, Telephone: 210-222-8449, Web site: <www.wingspress.com>

Index

C

D

J

K

L

M

O

Q

R

T

U

V

Y

Z